Anne Voelckers Palumbo

THE
STAY-AT-HOME
MOM'S
SURVIVAL GUIDE

Illustrated by: Anne Voelckers Palumbo

Edited by: Laurie Boucke and Linda Carlson

WHITE
BOUCKE
PUBLISHING
LAFAYETTE, COLORADO

First Published September 1997

Reprinted (with corrections) December 1998,
June 1999, February 2002, May 2006.

Printed in U.S.A.

Library of Congress Cataloging-in-Publication Data
Palumbo, Anne Voelckers.
    The stay-at-home moms survival guide / Anne Voelckers Palumbo ;
edited by Laurie Boucke and Linda Carlson.
    p. cm.
    ISBN: 1-888580-05-4 (pbk.)
    1. Mothers–Humor. I. Boucke, Laurie. II. Carlson, Linda. III. Title.
    PN6231.M68P35   1997
    818'.5407--dc21   97-10761
                                                CIP

WHITE BOUCKE PUBLISHING
PO BOX 400, LAFAYETTE, CO 80026, USA

CONTENTS

INTRODUCTION

In the past, it was easy to stay home and raise your children. All you had to do was poke your head out the door and the world was your oyster. Support for your stay-at-home devotion was unanimous. Respect for your self-sacrificing efforts was free-flowing. And friendships throughout the neighborhood flourished. No, not many women "worked" back then, and those who did were considered irresponsible, if not . . . promiscuous.

But times have changed, haven't they?

More than half of all women work now, relegating all the moms who choose to stay home—the dinosaurs of today—to a dubious rung on society's ladder. And what a surprise that standing is! Here we are, raising the next generation of superstars, and we have no claim to fame. Here we are, trading pumps for Play-Doh, and our paycheck is peanuts. Here we are, sublimating dreams for diapers, and society thinks we're asleep at the wheel.

There's no question: Life for the Stay-at-Home Mom ain't the bowl of cherries it used to be. Believe me, I know, having taken the plunge not too long ago.

But it doesn't need to be the pits either. Far from it. You just need to know the ropes, and the answers to questions like:

- Is it possible to engage in an intelligent conversation when your impressive mega-vocabulary has dwindled to two words: "goo" and "ga"?

- What are the "Dos & Don'ts" to follow at your husband's office party?

- Is there proper "Repairman Etiquette" every mother should follow?

- Are there acceptable stay-at-home lies that you can confidently use without feeling a shred of guilt?

- Is there a faster way to make stay-at-home friends than, say, waiting around for years at the park?

This *Stay-at-Home Mom's Survival Guide* sheds light on these pressing questions and much more. It also gives every Stay-at-Home Mom what she deserves most: A GOOD LAUGH!

PART 1

EVERYTHING YOU ALWAYS
WANTED TO KNOW ABOUT
SELF-ESTEEM, ISOLATION,
AND GOING NOOGIES,
BUT WERE AFRAID TO ASK

CLOSE QUARTERS
OF THE
STAY-AT-HOME KIND

1.

ARE YOU TOUGH ENOUGH TO STAY HOME?

Staying home these days takes guts. Not any old kind of guts. But, as my adorable child would say, "great big gobs of greasy, grimy, gopher guts." Funny thing is, many people actually think staying home is a piece of cake, a day at the beach, an excuse not to work. How wrong they are! Staying home is tough, so tough, in fact, that most of the tough get going—right on back to work.

I did not get going. I stayed home and weathered the storm, leaving strewn bottles in my wake as I struggled to make sense of my new life, my new social standing, and my new, horizontal belly button.

My only regret was not knowing the lowdown from the get-go. If I had known, for example, that a mother's vocabulary shrinks faster than a cotton sweater, then maybe I wouldn't have felt so flustered all those times I was rooting around for lost words. Or if, for instance, I had been forewarned about the considerable isolation, then perhaps I would've taken the high road and refrained from chasing after the UPS man with a cup of coffee and a packet of Ding Dongs.

But that's me and that's past. The question now is YOU. Are you tough enough to stay home? Most likely—whether you've been home a while or are merely contemplating the move—you are. But if you want to make doubly sure, I suggest you review the eight most important considerations any new mom can make. If after reviewing them you can easily say, "No problem," then you are a good candidate for staying home to raise your baby. Congratulations. You're on your way.

1. **Understand that your self-esteem may spring a leak.** There's nothing like a smattering of positive reinforcement—whether we're talking a pat on the back, a glowing performance review, or a big juicy paycheck—to keep the old esteemero running full speed ahead, is there? But, alas, one of the drawbacks of staying home is the lack of concrete recognition. No one but your family thinks to praise you anymore (and even they often forget).

2. **Anticipate that your life could rival a monk's.** Outside of committing a heinous crime or living in a monastery, there are few life situations that can offer you the same quality of isolation that staying at home does. Moms from coast to coast (especially the ones who live in rural areas with scary windchill factors) can attest to this grueling

fact. On the bright side, however, at least we—unlike the monks—can drive, talk, and even chew gum.

3. **Prepare for a society that pooh-poohs your efforts.** Our society is a fickle lot. They can't say enough about the importance of "family." They can't keep quiet about "quality time." They can't button up about the benefits of "bonding." But bring them face-to-face with the dedicated souls who actually practice what they preach and a funny thing happens: They look at you sideways; they question the contents of your brain, they mark you for someone who lolls around all day. Go figure.

4. **Bid old friends and coworkers a hasty adieu.** Everyone knows that once you become a parent, all of your friendships dry up faster than you could sing, "All they were was dust in the wind." You'd think friends and loyal coworkers would want to hear more about the color of your baby's stool, about the frightening depth of her cradle cap, about the nanosecond her umbilical cord dropped off, but no, they apparently do not.

5. **Embrace your new wardrobe staple: Sweats.** No, no, no! Not sweats! It's a common sentiment among new moms who have spent the last nine months in stretchy knits. But what's the alternative? Uncomfortably tight wool pants that chafe your waist? Hardly. Big, comfy, waist-forgiving sweats are the answer. Accept them, work with them, enjoy them. Besides, men have been languishing in them for years; it's our turn.

6. **Acknowledge that your vocabulary may dwindle.** Of all the considerations, this one is pretty tough to swallow. And for good reason. The idea of losing all those big, impressive, multisyllabic words that suggest *savoir faire*

is a horrifying one. But, sure enough, one morning you'll wake up unable to retrieve the simplest word, and it will dawn on you that the mechanics of your mind could use a tad more oil.

7. **Your relationship with The Big Guy may change.** Who knows exactly why, but becoming completely and totally financially dependent on a man tends to change things in the marital arena, occasionally transforming quite strong-willed women into docile weenie wives. Perhaps being put in one of life's most groveling positions—asking for cash—just might have something to do with it.

8. **Get set to get B-O-R-E-D.** Though most mothers are reluctant to admit it, staying home can be surprisingly dull. Not always, of course. But in between those exhilarating moments of sheer new-mom joy, there's lots of monotonous stuff to wear you down: carpet stains, clothing stains, crib stains, pet stains—and then, of course, repeated calls from your busybody mother-in-law with suggestions about how to get rid of all those exasperating stains.

Okay, so those are some of things every Stay-at-Home Mom needs to consider. No one said it was going to be easy but, hey, no one said that any of us has to totally succumb to the impositions either. The key here is *anticipation*, as in anticipating that you'll be asked over and over again: "What on earth do you do all day anyway, ya lazy lug?"

Read on for ways to stay tough as nails in situations that seem to unglue even the hardiest Stay-at-Home Moms.

2.

HOW TO PUT THE "STEAM" BACK IN YOUR SELF-ESTEEM

I'll never forget the day my self-esteem headed south. I was shopping with my cranky three-month-old, when I spotted the find of a lifetime: a sweatshirt the intoxicating color of "spittle." Knowing that I had but seconds left before my kid exploded into a full-blown cryfest and knowing that I absolutely had to have an article of clothing that could camouflage baby barf, I raced to the register with my sapling tucked under my arm. Before I could toss my wrinkled dollars on the counter, a well-dressed woman with a briefcase (a Working Woman, no doubt) tossed her dainty purchase (a silk top, what else?) and her corporate credit card right over my deeply discounted, oatmeal-colored, weeks-without-washing sweatshirt.

Who do you think the salesperson waited on? Yes, you are correct. Not me! Okay, okay, so I forgot to comb my hair. And, oh, all right, I was wearing pajamas under my coat. But the fact remains, I was there first, and yet the ungrateful thing waited on *her* over me, giving me the distinct impression that the Working Woman's time and money were more important than my own.

Slinking out, with my head hung lower than a lizard's, I questioned why I allowed either of those felines to shoo me aside. Was it because my baby's cries were setting off the store alarm? Or was it because I no longer felt like a highly respected, every-hair-in-place working professional?

"Chin up," a stay-at-home veteran advised me, "your self-esteem's about to be put through the ringer now that you're a full-time mom. And that incident in the store was just the beginning."

"J ... J ... Just the beginning?" I stammered in disbelief.

"Let me put it to you this way," she said. "Your new place of employment isn't exactly what you'd call 'esteem building.' Think about it. Jeans with ground-in graham crackers is the dress code. 'Wee Sing' has replaced Muzak. Your coffee break never ends. A paycheck is out of the question. And your coworkers are unable to read . . . let alone walk, talk, or feed themselves."

I saw her point. In a remarkably short period of time, I had indeed gone from making dough to baking dough, from impressing superiors to wiping posteriors, from balancing budgets to balancing blocks, from doing spreadsheets to assembling car seats.

She continued, "And don't be alarmed if you suddenly find yourself begging your speechless, hairless, clueless baby for a compliment. It's okay to want a shred of recognition; and since your baby is the most likely candidate to give it, I say GO FOR IT."

Words of wisdom on the "reality" of staying home are hard to come by. Mostly, all we ever hear about are the rewards: the bonding, the first smile, the first step, the irretrievable years. And while the rewards are often phenomenal, they don't really thwart that I'm-not-feeling-so-good-about-myself feeling.

What does? I asked some veteran Stay-at-Home Moms, and this is what they recommended:

Take a Continuing Education class . . .

> If not for the mental challenge, then for the contact with human beings over 20 inches tall, with teeth, a full head of hair, and who don't smell like they need to be changed.

Discard the archaic notion that "house cleaning" is a worthwhile endeavor . . .

> It's not and it never will be. Rather than pursue thankless chores specifically designed to make you cry out, "I can't take this anymore," choose to pursue a meaningful hobby.

Inspect the closets of other Stay-at-Home Moms . . .

> Discovering that others have closets crammed full of unfinished projects and scattered baby photos will give you goose pimples of satisfaction.

Plant your feet a yard apart when asking hubby for cash . . .

> This military stance has been proven to negate any foolish feelings associated with this humbling task. Then be sure to spend it all on yourself.

Imbed tacks in the soles of your sneakers . . .

Nothing beats the authoritative click of a Mom-on-the-Move.

Read! Read! Read!

An informed mother is a respected mother. Besides, it gives you something to talk about other than your sagging appendages.

Get out of the house each and every day . . .

Leaving the premises forces you to comb your hair and change your clothes—activities that may otherwise get overlooked.

Embrace rewards as they come . . .

A false-alarm diaper; a to-kill-for parking spot in the pouring rain; a big, sloppy kiss planted smack on your right eye. Though inconsequential to some, they can jump-start a mother's self-esteem back to life.

Make friends with other Stay-at-Home Moms . . .

Just knowing there are other moms bouncing off the walls is one of the biggest self-esteem boosters of all. You're not alone.

Memorize good comebacks to dreaded questions . . .

Practice them daily! Unleash them with gusto! And never leave home without them. (Cat got your tongue? See the next chapter for some sizzling retorts.)

3.

QUICK COMEBACKS TO IRRITATING QUESTIONS

Of all the esteem-building tips I was given, mastering quick comebacks to birdbrained questions literally catapulted my self-esteem into the next galaxy. Granted, it took me years to sharpen this skill, but it was worth the effort.

Take a look at the questions. If you haven't been asked most of them already, chances are you'll be asked some of them in the near future. And chances are also that you'll resent the *cross-examiner* because:

1. The person is a *woman*.

2. She seems hell-bent on undermining your stay-at-home life.

3.   You didn't have an appropriate response.

But what exactly is an appropriate response? Well, it all depends on what kind of day you're having, how bloated you're feeling, who you're talking to, and whether or not you plan to ever talk to this person again. Each situation is different, so you'll have to be the judge.

If, for example, I'm having an unusually great day—one where my little butterball takes a record-breaking nap—then I always use the confident responses categorized as "polite," no matter who's doing the asking.

But if I am having the worst possible day in the world—one that starts with my mother-in-law screeching, "How can you live in this pigsty?" and ends with her yelling, "I always knew my son could do better than YOU!"—then I am unable to stop myself from using the rather cruel responses labeled "nasty."

If I'm having a mildly annoying day (one where I crack my head on the side of the car every time I buckle butterball in), then I always feel compelled to stick it to 'em with the noticeably "perturbed" comebacks . . . unless, of course, the person asking is responsible for something significant like, say, my husband's paycheck or my child's report card. In those cases, I bite my tongue and painfully resort to the "polite" responses.

Will you return to work?

Polite:	Not in the near future. I'm content being home now.
Perturbed:	Return to work? This *is* my work!
Nasty:	Did you say, "Return to work" or "Realign your nose?"

What do you DO all day?

Polite:	I never stop. It's go-go-go from sunup to sundown. But I love it!
Perturbed:	That's for me to know and for you to never find out.
Nasty:	I sleep, I watch TV, and inhale bonbons. Satisfied?

How can you bear not making any money?

Polite:	It's an adjustment, but it won't last forever.
Perturbed:	It's a killer! I feel so worthless! Money was my identity!
Nasty:	After day-care expenses, what do *you* make? About a buck an hour?

Don't you feel like your mind is turning to mush?

Polite:	Thankfully, no. I read quite a lot.
Perturbed:	I don't get the question.
Nasty:	(A big burp should be sufficient.)

Don't your kids drive you nuts?

Polite:	Not my kids. They're terrific!
Perturbed:	No. Unlike *some* mothers I know, I actually wanted *my* kids.
Nasty:	They used to, but now I chain them to their beds all day.

Don't you feel subservient to your husband?

Polite: Of course not! He admires the sacrifices I've made.

Perturbed: No way! It's the dog who wears the pants in our family.

Nasty: Yes, we like it that way. He's the master and I'm his little genie.

Don't you regret letting your career slip away?

Polite: My home is my career.

Perturbed: Gee, your sudden interest in my career is truly touching. Truly. I'll keep you posted.

Nasty: Say what? I was mesmerized by your pumps. Where'd ya find those gigantic things anyway?

How can you stand being cooped up at home all day?

Polite: Believe me, I get out every day.

Perturbed: Well, after I make a few prank phone calls, I typically give myself a great big wedgie.

Nasty: Stand it? I'd say it's a helluva lot better than being cooped up in some 3' x 3' office cell.

Could you watch my kids after school?

Polite: Sorry. My hands are full as it is.

Perturbed: Why on earth would I want to?

Nasty: Your kids? I'd rather lie naked on a red anthill.

Do you drink during the day?

Polite: Oh, come on . . . of course not.

Perturbed: Yes, and I entertain men, too.

Nasty: What a thoughtful and caring question. And I thought you were just an insensitive clod.

4.

THE
STAY-AT-HOME
SELF-ESTEEM TEST

Is your self-esteem on shaky ground? Take this test and see for yourself whether you need to pump a little steam back into that self-esteem of yours.

		True	False
1.	I sleep in my clothes and wear them the next day.	___	___
2.	Chain letters scare the daylights out of me; I always obey them lest I'll be struck by lightening.	___	___

		True	**False**
3.	When I stand next to a Working Woman, I find myself mysteriously shrinking.	_____	_____
4.	I typically replace the words "I'm furious" with "I'm sorry."	_____	_____
5.	I often raise my hand to speak.	_____	_____
6.	I now stand pigeon-toed.	_____	_____
7.	Being able to change a messy diaper in under a minute makes me feel special.	_____	_____
8.	I wish construction workers would pay more attention to me.	_____	_____
9.	The mere sound of a ringing phone sends me into paroxysms of grateful joy.	_____	_____
10.	I love the word "just," as in: I'm *just* a housewife, *just* a mom, *just* a slave to my kids.	_____	_____
11.	When people compliment me, I burst into tears and scream, "You're lying!"	_____	_____
12.	I cut my own hair.	_____	_____

SCORING:

For each "false," give yourself 10 points. No points for "true" answers. If your score is:

Over 100 — Holy Prudential! Your self-esteem must be chiseled from the Rock of Gibraltar. If I may take a brief moment to speak on behalf of all Stay-at-Home Moms, I'd just like to say, "WE'RE GREEN WITH ENVY."

60 to 90 — You're doing great! Be sure to share your self-esteem-building tips with the rest of us. (Mum's the word, however, if "housecleaning" is the key to your high self-esteem. Ugh-o. Give us something juicy we can sink our teeth into.)

20 to 50 — Your self-esteem could definitely use a good shot in the arm. I suggest you throw down that *Parents* magazine, flip on some tunes, and do the Macarena. Hey, there's nothing like a little dancing to make you feel alive.

0 or 10 — Considering your vulnerable state, let me just say . . . well, on second thought, I don't think I'll say anything. Why pour salt on an open wound. Not that you're an open wound or that you even like salt. What I mean is . . . oh, never mind.

5.

ISOLATION: TOO MUCH OF IT CAN DRIVE YOU NOOGIES

The question I am asked most often by new, nervous, and prospective mothers wondering about life in the sorta-slow-stay-at-home lane is this: "Do you feel isolated staying home?"

"Yes!" I shout from my underground world of nookies, binkies, and num-nums. "I feel shut off from the outside world. But that's okay. My baby and I need this time to bond and, by golly, we're bonding. Come to think of it, I've bonded with more than just the baby. Otis, our dog, and I seem to have renewed our love. Chelsea, our cat, seems to be using her litter box more. And even the washing machine seems a lot more cooperative."

The second question they ask is, "HOW CAN YOU STAND IT?"

Well, I must confess, it's been an adjustment. Oh, okay, it's been the biggest whopping adjustment of my entire life, bigger, even, than learning how to share a bathroom with my one and only.

It wouldn't be so bad, I think, if there were gangs of moms banging down my door each morning for some adult conversation and coffee. (Hey, I'd even welcome gangs of bikers at this point.) But no one's around. Nobody just drops in anymore. And no matter how hard I try, I can't get the gas-and-electric man to come in for some Teddy Grahams and cocoa.

Slowly but surely, however, I've made peace with my new lifestyle and, in doing so, have found special ways to entertain the new, more introspective me. "What ways?" you're dying to know. Well, for instance, I love to see how long my cat can run with a banana peel on its head. When I was working I never had time for silly stuff like that. And I really enjoy tossing a ball at the bird feeder and watching the birds scatter. The commotion that follows always makes me feel so ALIVE!

Of course, there are days when I go too far, like the day I put a wig on my baby as a surrogate for adult companionship. That was funny up until the moment my husband walked in, knocked on my head, and said, "I think you need to get out a little more, Ms. Plath."

And he was right. My cubs and I had been hanging in the old abode from sunup to sundown; and we'd been doing it for weeks: stacking blocks, knocking 'em over, stacking 'em up again, and finally pitching a few at the dog who was too happy for his own good. Who knows what would've happened if I hadn't made a concerted effort right then to smooth my feathers and leave my cozy nest?

Well, actually, I do know what would have happened. I would have succumbed to the dreaded Stockholm syndrome, that thing that happens to prisoners who have been kept in dark, isolated cells for months on end. After a while, they become listless . . . dependent . . . passive. Yes, they become, through no fault of their own, cooped-up, goofed-up, stay-at-home-alone screwballs!

You, of course, want to steer clear of this syndrome. It's true, isolation does have its benefits, allowing you to bond with animate and inanimate objects alike. But too much of it can be a bad thing.

So how do you prevent yourself from becoming over-isolated? It's easy. You simply take the following "Am-I-Going-Noogies?" Quiz from time to time or, depending on your state of mind, from hour to hour. Your score will let you know in a flash if you've been entombed a tad too long.

6.

THE OFFICIAL AM-I-GOING-NOOGIES? QUIZ

1. Every morning, you watch your sharply dressed neighbor zoom off to work. This makes you:

   A. Wonder if she misses her kids during the day.

   B. Hope she misses her kids during the day.

   C. Pray her kids will be deranged as adults.

   D. Sob uncontrollably: My God how you miss accessories and separates!

2. A big furniture truck is in the driveway of a new neighbor. You:

   A. Notice it and go about your business.

   B. Peek jealously from behind the curtains.

   C. Call and ask the following: what's being delivered, how much it costs, and how on earth they can afford it?

   D. March over, help the strapping delivery men carry the couch in and then invite them over for a slice of cheesecake.

3. When a friend suggests your baby is fat, you:

   A. Consider her remark and lay off the crackers.

   B. Retaliate by saying, "Well, your baby is bald!"

   C. Rush your baby to the nearest Trauma Center and demand a complete muscle-to-fat analysis.

   D. Clutch her throat with a pair of spaghetti tongs and hiss, "Take it back. Now!"

4. When you reach the "Mother's Occupation" section of any form, you:

   A. Leave it blank.

   B. Begrudgingly write, "Homemaker."

   C. Notice symptoms of a near-professional death experience and hypnotically fill in "Neurosurgeon."

D.   Roll up the form and swat the nearest victim, screaming, "There is no name for what I do! I am an unsung hero!"

5.   When your husband comes home from work, you:

   A.   Give him a quick kiss and continue making dinner.

   B.   Dropkick the baby into his arms and flee out the front door.

   C.   Leech onto his leg, refusing to let go as he drags you from room to room.

   D.   Tie him up with electrical tape and torture irrelevant office gossip out of him.

6.   When you hear the mail truck coming down the road, you:

   A.   Notice it but continue feeding your baby.

   B.   Steel yourself against the desire to bolt and wait five torturous minutes before you sashay down to the mailbox.

   C.   Leap tall trees to reach the mail truck and hungrily snatch the day's mail because it's your only link to life.

   D.   Run after the truck, hop in, and say, "Let's go to Rio, babycakes!"

7.   The telephone has not rung all day. You:

   A.   Call any friend who happens to be home and unload.

   B.   Call your husband and pathetically ask, "Why haven't you callllled?"

C.   Slump into the nearest chair, convinced you have no life, no friends, no heartbeat.

D.   Rip the phone out of the wall and heave it at the cat.

8. When you reach the "weddings" section of the local newspaper, you:

A.   Ignore it; you've got better things to read.

B.   Peruse it quickly, looking mainly at where the couples honeymooned.

C.   Play a game whereby you try to guess the bride's occupation by how much cleavage is showing.

D.   Spend hours analyzing each couple: Why is he looking off? Are her breasts real? Will the marriage last if he's as goofy as he looks?

9. You overhear a neighbor's voice on your Fisher-Price monitor. You:

A.   Simply switch it off.

B.   Listen long enough to assess whether or not she's a good parent.

C.   Strap the monitor to your ear, put your feet up, and wait for the juicy tidbits to come home to mama.

D.   Scream "FIRE" into the monitor just for cruel kicks.

10. A gigantic dustball has collected in the corner. This makes you:

   A.   Do nothing. After all, dustballs are magnets for other dust.

   B.   Pick it up the second you're finished sorting socks.

   C.   Flog yourself for ever letting it collect in the first place.

   D.   Call the exterminator. You're positive the thing moved. Or was that a ghost?

11. When a good friend asks you to join the gang for a "Mom's-Night-Out," you:

   A.   Scream: "Yes! Yes! A thousand times YES!"

   B.   Say you'll think about it and get back to her.

   C.   Say "no" because you need to disinfect the diaper pail.

   D.   Shout: "And leave my baby? Whaddaya think, I'm some kinda hussy?"

12. When you pass by a mirror during the day, you:

   A.   Take a quick look and brush your bangs back.

   B.   Pinch your skin taut to see what a face-lift would look like.

   C.   Recite again the conversation you plan to have with your neighbors about their annoying dog.

D.   Practice sexy growls and gyrations Madonna-
style.

SCORING

For each A answer, award yourself 10 points. For each B, give yourself 5 points. For each C, give yourself 1 point. Sorry, no points for D.

Over 90 — Bravo! You've somehow managed to withstand the wear and tear of a life behind drywall and siding. Keep up the good work.

36 to 90 — You're hovering in a risky zone here. That cork could blow any minute unless you make a concerted effort to connect with the human race.

6 to 35 — You are one cell away from experiencing a full-blown case of the Stockholm syndrome. GET OUT OF THE HOUSE NOW!

0 to 5 — Repeat after me, "I-am-not-under-house-arrest. I-have-committed-no-crime. I-am-free-to-go."

PART 2

DON'T LEAVE HOME
WITHOUT IT!

THE
STAY-AT-HOME
BRAIN

7.

WHO PUT THE DRAIN-O IN MY BRAIN-O?

It's a frightening feeling to wake up one morning and discover that while you were asleep part of your brain went permanently to sleep.

That's what happened to me, or rather, to the word-retrieval unit of my brain. I knew something was amiss when I couldn't think of the word "refrigerator." I kept saying to my husband who was holding the milk, "Uh, uh, put it in the, uh, uh, you know, that big white box. Uh, uh, oh, that big appliance that smells."

"Cracked a book lately?" he asked, his eyes saucer-sized with concern.

The thing is, I had cracked a book lately, many a book: *Kitten Finds a Mitten; Teddy Wets His Beddy;* and *Toady's Got a Loady.* But those books didn't seem to help at all. In fact, they probably contributed to the daily word struggle that rendered me speechless as a clam.

Had something else caused my once-impressive 20,000-word vocabulary to dwindle to an unimpressive two words: "goo" and "ga?" Why, yes, of course! Many things had. Never logging more than an hour of uninterrupted sleep had definitely put a chink in the old cerebral armor. Scant contact with the outside world couldn't be viewed as a plus. All those raspberries I'd been blowing had undeniably swollen my tongue to a size incapable of articulation. And who knows, maybe big-fat-Barney was the big-fat-culprit in more ways than one.

Sooner or later, you'll probably find yourself in the same boat, struggling for words as common as "crib." But don't fret. It's only natural, and thank God, only temporary. Once you start sleeping and reading and ordering items over the phone again, those great big words will flood right back in, especially the great big swear words.

In the meantime, however, you'll need to pretend that everything's running smoothly upstairs, that's right, *pretend.* Otherwise, people will think you've gone soft. And who needs that? Certainly not you. No way! What you need to feel is on top of the game.

How do you fake it? You follow my six easy steps for holding an intelligent conversation when you are feeling, ahem, language-impaired. I know they work because (1) I have successfully used them and (2) Big Cheese Executives with limited vocabularies use them all the time.

8.

HOW TO HOLD AN INTELLIGENT CONVERSATION WITH AN "ITSY-BITSY" VOCABULARY

STEP 1

Lower your octave. All those "so bigs" and "gootchy goos" have elevated your voice to a pitch only dogs and babies can hear. Consider which sounds more intelligent: "I'm on the brink of a discovery" in a chipmunk voice or, "I've discovered the gene-marker for bed-wetting" in your best Lauren Bacall?

STEP 2

Sprinkle your conversational feedback with lots of "well, wells" and "I sees" and "indeeds." These 10-cent phrases give the impression you're intelligently tuned in when, in fact, your mind may be on more important matters, such as . . . where's that funky smell coming from?!

STEP 3

Yawn and look away. This unnerving gesture lets you off the hook by making the talkers feel so boring that they begin rambling incoherently. Note: This is a particularly good technique to use when you're so tired you can't even form a sentence, let alone stand.

STEP 4

Squeeze as many "ate-ending" words into your dialogue as possible: inundate, ruminate, incarcerate, obliterate, irritate. Who cares if they make sense or not in the context of the conversation? You can always count on the "ate" words to up your perceived IQ by at least 20 points.

STEP 5

Knit your brow and feverishly nod your head. You might even try crossing your arms and occasionally stomping your foot. Hey, this body language has worked for lots of presidents—and it can work for you, too.

STEP 6

Suck a lemon. This should reduce the size of your tongue, allowing for crisp articulation once again. After all, it's not what you say, it's how well you say it.

9.

ONE MOTHER'S LANGUAGE DETERIORATION OVER A TEN-YEAR SPAN

(As told to me by Susan Green)

My philosophy has always been, if you know what you're up against, you know what you're up against. So before I decided to stay home, I wanted to know what might happen to my illustrious language skills.

Amazingly, I found a mother who had been home for a decade and who was willing to share her story. Lucky ducky me. I mean, how terribly fortunate I was to have located such a willing candidate. Her case history follows:

Year 1

Some language usage still existed. I purposely used words like "eschew," "belittle," and "serendipitous" just to show the world that having a baby hadn't zapped my mind.

Year 2:

My language skills dropped off sharply. No two-syllable words could be heard coming from my slack jaw. My favorite words were "no" and "don't."

Year 3:

I routinely called friends "silly ducks" and ended the majority of words with the suffixes "roo" and "ette" as in: "Let's take a little strollaroo around the blockette."

Year 4:

Whenever my husband asked me if I wanted to go out to dinner, I typically replied: "Me no wanna go."

Year 5:

All of my sentences rhymed. I would say things like: "I'm going to the store, be back at four. I'll buy some meat, for us to eat. It'll taste so good, like I knew it woooooooould."

Year 6:

On a lark, I took the *Reader's Digest* "It Pays to Enrich Your Word Power" quiz. Frighteningly, I scored a big Mother Goose egg.

Year 7:

My child asked me how to spell the word "once." I replied: "W-O-N-C-E." Later I thought, "What a funny word, 'wonce'." Wonder what it means?

Year 8:

I renamed all my children "Hey-you" and discovered that the words I used most often were: whatchamacallit, thingamabob, and whoozamajiggy.

Year 9:

My subject-verb agreement was completely shot, causing me to ask such questions as, "Where is my shoes?"

Year 10:

A banner year! Impressive words started to return, but correct usage was hit or miss—as in, having my hair "truncated," my tax forms "copulated," and the "carbuncle" fixed on my car.

10.

THE BEST DARN BRAIN ADVICE A MOTHER CAN OFFER

All kidding aside, I really haven't noticed a marked decrease in my brainpower since I've been home. When I worked, all I thought about were the weekends, and the same goes for life now.

Oh sure, I can't always come up with a particular word the moment I want to, but give me an hour and I'll produce "amnesia." And true, my memory without Post-It notes is like the earth without gravity. But for the most part, it's still the same reliable brain, chugging along, collecting all sorts of useful, useless, and disgusting information.

So, no, staying home does not turn your brain into a great big old cotton ball. That comes later. What it does do, however, is make you feel like things are a little breezier up there than they were before.

My advice to you? Try your hardest not to poke fun at your brain, especially in public, and definitely not within a one-mile radius of a Working Woman. There's simply no need to share the fact that, say, you can't remember who discovered America with the all-too-eager-to-hear world. Remember, the condition is only temporary.

Here are just a few of the self-deprecating comments you should avoid at all cost:

My mind has turned to mush.

There's a geranium in my cranium.

I'm one Pamper short of a 12-pak.

My brain has fallen and it can't get up.

_____ (Fill in your favorite.)

11.

HOW TO GET AN ADVANCED STAY-AT-HOME DEGREE

Wouldn't it be great if all the time we spent wipin' bottoms, singin' lullabies, sortin' socks, zippin' coats, spreadin' peanut butter, ticklin' tummies, and kissin' boo-boos translated into an advanced degree—like a master's in Domestic Engineering?

We could all walk just a tad taller, secure in the knowledge that we were earning credits for such mundane activities as standing around at the playground watching our children play.

And if we ever decided to return to work, we could slap that degree on our resume and proclaim we earned it through "Home Study."

Here are some of the courses we might take for our advanced stay-at-home degree; that is, if there ever were such a glorious thing.

How to Start-Stop, Start-Stop a Project

Experience the joy of accumulating unfinished projects. From botched throw pillows to half-painted walls to neglected photo albums, this course covers the fundamentals of task initiation, procrastination, stagnation, resignation, cessation, and finally, resurrection. Emphasis placed on how to leave things at loose ends without blowing a mental gasket.

Materials needed: One dorky craft project you'd just as soon ignore.

Introduction to Pet Stores

This course has been designed for unsuspecting moms who, for lack of anything better to do, have been thrust into the disgusting arena of pet stores.

Topics include: Overcoming hostility to the store's mascot parrot when it won't say your child's name; suppressing the urge to gag near the dog cages; enduring the ear-splitting cackle of one million birds; pronouncing the name of every fish in every tank in every aisle without strangling your toddler; and communicating with a possessed breed of salesperson that speaks only in animal tongue.

Conversational Baby Talk

Here it is! The course all mothers who still speak in complete sentences have been dying to take. Learn how to create your own language by making up such meaningful words as "zatsagoodboopie" and discover the incredibly annoying joy of talking in a high-pitched, sing-songy voice.

This course also covers the meaning of such advanced sentence structures as "goo-goo-ga-ga-anna-goo-ga-da-vida-baby" and stresses the importance of blowing raspberries during pauses.

Surgeon General Warning: Practicing baby talk around other adults has been found to be extremely hazardous to your social life.

Standing Around with Dignity

Since the dawn of time, women have been standing around, watching their offspring develop at a snail's pace. The key to this age-old activity, however, is doing it with dignity. Sound challenging? Relax! This course makes it a snap by teaching such techniques as "gnarly brow knitting" to give the impression that serious thinking is occurring; "mad pacing" to suggest you're on the brink of some huge discovery; and "repetitive hand wringing" to imply you've got big things going on the burner back home.

Clothes Shopping with a Toddler

All those ugly clothes getting you down? Discover the thrill of shopping with a toddler in tow. Certified instructors come right to your house to train you in the sophisticated techniques of dodging a toppling mannequin, reassembling a pulled-down clothes rack, locating a child amidst a sweater landslide, pretending the child sniffing the lingerie is not really yours, and handling such rude remarks as, "Get your bleeping brat out of my dressing stall!" Prerequisite: One horse-sized Valium.

Toilet Co-Dependency

Do you feel anxious and guilty when your toilet is dirty? Bored and restless when it's clean? Congratulations! You're on the fast track to becoming one with your johnny. This course, designed to wring the most out of your co-dependency, focuses on taking your toilet's flush personally, overcommitting to thruway rest stops, seeking out particularly abusive toilets, and tolerating scum buildup to avoid latrine backlash.

Foul-Odor Appreciation

Orson Welles once said, "I will taste no wine before its time." Take heart, odor aficionados, the same can be said for household smells. In the flutter of a nostril, learn how to wallow in the complex yet revolting bouquets of mangy socks, nasty diaper pails, rancid sponges, week-old bathing suits, gag'em sneakers, rotting leftovers, putrid pet cages, and—that oldie but goodie—vomit. Note: Mothers with prior sniffing experience are advised to blend two or more noxious fumes to torque their nose holes to maximum capacity.

Playing Horsey

A funny thing happens when you become a parent—you also become a horse. Or at least that's what kiddies think when they hop on and shout, "Giddy up, you old saw!" This course, designed by the Horse Whisperer himself, teaches parents how to buck toddlers without cracking a rib, as well as ways to whinny without drooling. Parents also learn the telltale signs of when to slow down (gasping for air), when to stop (irregular heartbeat), and when to never play horsey again (permanent nerve damage in neck).

Living with Stains

Learn to love your stains! Unlike so many Heloise-type courses that focus on stain removal, this course motivates moms to accept their stains for all they're worth. Using a series of deep-breathing and biofeedback techniques, moms discover how to (1) not move a muscle when Tang spills on her white carpet; (2) freeze when Junior tracks in tar; and (3) go limp when the baby spits up Hawaiian Punch all over her new silk blouse.

Catalog Addiction

Imagine, in just three short months you could be a full-fledged catalog addict. This course reveals in spine-tingling detail how to get on every list from Lillian Vernon to Gumps. Other topics include:

- Catalog anticipation (how many will I get today?).

- Production frustration (nothing ever fits!).

- Catalog snobbery (oh, I thought you got *Hammacher Schlemmer . . .*)

- Returned-goods denial (let's see, I spent over $100 on return postage, and have nothing to show for it, but that's okay, I guess . . . right?)

PART 3

LOVE MEANS NEVER HAVING TO SAY, "I'M SORRY I RAN OVER YOUR GOLF CLUBS IN A FIT OF RAGE, HONEYBUN."

THE SPOUSAL UNIT

12.

HE'S HIP, YOU'RE HIP, BUT NOW THAT YOU'RE HOME FULL TIME . . .

I t's 5:05. Do you know where your husband is? Yikes! You do! He's on his way home, expecting all kinds of spectacular things. A toy-free driveway. A delicious, hot meal. A floor sans goo. Happy kids, excited to see him. Easily located mail. A picked-up home. And a cheerful wife with combed hair.

What does he get? Well, for starters, none of the above. The driveway is a catastrophe of toys. The delicious, hot meal consists of reheated linguine. The floor, caked with Kool-Aid, snags one of his loafers. The fighting kids are oblivious to his arrival. The mail is "Oh, here, somewhereee." The house looks tornado-struck, and you . . . YOU. Where exactly shall we begin?

After heaving the screaming baby into your husband's arms with a curt, "Your turn," you collapse into the nearest chair, releasing a colossal sigh.

"Another bad day?" he mumbles as babykins is gently dumped back in your lap.

"Horrendous," you groan, wedging the kicking baby back into his armpit.

"Maybe it's time you, you know, got a part-time job," he suggests as he always does whenever you've had a particularly gruesome day.

"B . . . b . . . but I don't want to get a part-time job," you snort. "It's just that, that, that, that I HAVEN'T TALKED TO ANOTHER ADULT ALL DAY!"

Now it's his turn to release a colossal sigh, which he does because he knows what's next. He must painfully recount in excruciating detail his entire day: his meetings, what he had for lunch, what his secretary wore, the new carpet, the receptionist's pregnancy . . . and so on.

Perched on the edge of your chair, unaware of your pathetic demeanor, you soak up his inane ramblings with the fervor of a starving puppy. Upon completion of the inquest, he inadvertently pats your head while you quite consciously lick his hand.

Staying at home will shift, if not rock, the foundation of even the best marriages. Things simply change when you're home all day meeting the never-ending needs of small children and repulsive pets.

It's not that he doesn't respect you; heck, he was the one who supported your desire to stay home in the first place. It's not that he doesn't find you intelligent; no, you remind him hourly of your towering IQ. It's not that he doesn't find you attractive; why, just this morning he remarked how those dark circles under your eyes make you look mysterious. And it's not that he doesn't find you interesting; who wouldn't find your enthusiastic recaps of Kathie Lee, Rosie, and Oprah captivating?

It's that the balance of power undeniably shifts when you stay at home. Although neither of you would ever admit that your relationship is a throwback in time—where he's the mighty warrior bringing home the bacon and you're the self-sacrificing underling stoking the home fires—you've got to admit there have been occasions when you thought he said, "Me, Tarzan, thirsty. You, Jane, go fetchum brewski root."

HOW TO HOLD YOUR OWN (NOT *HIS*, SILLY!)

So what do you do with these feelings of inferiority . . . these feelings that arouse monumental guilt when the heating bill is off the charts . . . these feelings that trigger night-long pouts when his secretary calls after hours . . . these feelings that stop you from asking for a little more help?

It's simple. You use these feelings as "warning flags" for reshifting the balance of power back to YOU.

It's not: "Honey, do you, um, think I could have 12 little dollars, for, um, a pair of marked-down shoes from the '80s?"

It's: "I need $50 for a pair of designer slingbacks and I need it now!"

It's not: "Sweetie, do you suppose that maybe just maybe you could change munchkin's diaper? My arm is broken."

It's: "Hey, lazybones. Munchy's got a load. Change it!"

It's not: "Darling, I've been feeling so ugly lately. I was wondering if you could reassure me that—although I've lost most of my hair and my body is covered with dry, scaly patches and I'm suffering from unmentionable digestion—you still find me somewhat attractive?"

It's: "All in favor of saying mom looks like a million bucks, say 'AYE'!"

Get the picture? Then let them hear you R-O-A-R.

13.

MOTHER ALERT: TOP TEN WARNING SIGNS YOU'RE BECOMING A WEENIE WIFE

YOU . . .

1. Gleefully agree to a week's vacation at the Baseball Hall of Fame.

2. Buy him a LA-Z-BOY and lovingly watch him sleeping in it all weekend long.

3. Shower him with praise for coming home before midnight.

4. Iron his boxers and stack them by color.

5. Beg his permission to let you wash and wax his car.

6. Can't say enough about that one bolt he tightened on the garage door, "Why, you could build houses, you great big He-Man!"

7. Scrape the grass out of his golf-shoe cleats and then set up ten "tee times" in a row.

8. Call him "Sarge."

9. Ask him over and over again, "Why, darling, are you losing weight?"

10. Mow the lawn with a rusty push-mower and think that's just peachy keen.

14.

GETTING THE LUMMOX
TO LIFT A FINGER

Asking your mate to help a little more around the house is not only a universal problem among Stay-at-Home Moms, it's akin to asking a two-ton sheep dog to move off a toasty heat vent. Neither will budge without a colossal reward.

Some mothers, usually the ones with angels hanging all over the place, are reluctant to ask because they feel morally tied to their chores. Other mothers, the ones raised with "guilt" as their guiding light, are hesitant to ask because they feel guilty not bringing in any money. And then all the other mothers, the ones who initially expected a little help goddamnit, are disinclined to ask anymore because, quite miraculously, their mates have gone stone-cold deaf whenever they have requested a little assistance.

What this means is that you, as a respectable person, have to make a decision: Are you going to work your knuckles to the bone as you tackle every single household chore in seething silence? Or are you going to make the commitment it takes—in time, in effort, and in begging—to get your man to pitch in around the palace?

I have tried both ways, and trust me, getting some assistance from the Big Guy is better. Usually the straightforward approach works best:

I simply say, "I need you to take out the trash."

He replies, "What year?"

We laugh, then I hit him with a skillet and hand him the bag.

But that doesn't always work. There will be times when you'll need to use a less-than-straightforward approach. Here are some approaches for you to consider next time you want more help around the house:

THE STROKE-THE-EGO APPROACH

"Darling, could you please take out the surprisingly heavy trash? The job truly requires someone with sexy shirt-splitting muscles . . . someone like YOU."

THE SUBLIMINAL APPROACH

"StudMuffin, could you please *[sex tonight]* take out the *[sex tonight]* trash?"

THE MANIPULATIVE APPROACH

"Wow, am I tired! Not only did I drive 600 miles to get that spare part you wanted for the car, but I made it home in time to make Beef Wellington for dinner. Oh, by the way, would you please take out the trash?"

THE NEGATIVE APPROACH

"Sweetie, you wouldn't NOT take out the trash, would you?"

THE PASSIVE-AGGRESSIVE APPROACH

This approach requires no talking. All you do is plunk the greasy trash bag in his lap, smile sweetly, and walk away.

THE REVERSE-PSYCHOLOGY MARTYR APPROACH

"Darling, could you? Ah, what's the use. Just forget I was even going to ask you to take out the trash. You wouldn't anyway. You never do anything I want you to do."

THE NAIVE APPROACH

"Honey, would you look at this! Wow! I've never seen our trash container so full before. And, lookee there, there's mold growing on the side. Huh? Wonder how long it's been since we've emptied the trash? Think we'll catch a terminal disease?"

THE "IF-YOU, THEN-YOU'D" APPROACH

"*If you* loved me, *then you'd* take out the trash . . ."

    (or, more affirmatively)

"*If you* don't want me to wrap that 9-iron around your neck, *then you'd* better take out the trash!"

15.

DOS AND DON'TS OF YOUR HUSBAND'S OFFICE PARTY

Did you have a good time at hubby's office party? No, me neither. And it wasn't because I drank too much and called the Top Dog a Big Bowzer. I felt "dismissed," if you know what I mean, for not being an incredibly fascinating working person with hilarious elevator jokes.

You, however, can avoid feeling dismissed by following these simple suggestions:

DO brush up on relevant current events: our precarious health-care system, our weakened infrastructure, our frustrating foreign trade policy.

DON'T discuss your child's raging diaper rash and the gazillion creams you've used to cure it.

DO wear clothing that exudes self-confidence: anything bold, tailored, and apronless.

DON'T cinch an old pregnancy dress and slap on some baggy support hose.

DO laugh at sexual jokes, innuendoes, and anything else related to America's favorite topic.

DON'T lament loudly the last time you had sex and then bring up the worst word in the English language: episiotomy.

DO listen—just listen—when people are talking.

DON'T rearrange collars, pick off lint, inspect for lice, or tell someone they need a nap.

DO keep the discussion of your baby's amazing achievements to under a minute.

DON'T drag out baby books, progress charts or "day-one" baby pics that are, ahem, less photogenic than you think.

DO clap loudly when your husband receives an award for outstanding service.

DON'T hiss, "Ha! With all that dedication, you'd think he could change a diaper or two!"

DO muster some energy and shake your bootie.

DON'T succumb to the bone-crushing lethargy that has been with you since childbirth and sneak off to the coatroom for a quick nap.

DO eat your meal slowly, savoring every delicious bite prepared by someone other than you!

DON'T wolf down your meal standing up.

DO have terrific answers to that dreaded question: "So what's new with you?" Perk up and say something clever like, "I'm glad you asked. I'm working on an invention that improves men's hearing during the night. And you?"

DON'T mumble, "Nuthin'."

PART 4

SEX! LIES! GUILT! TEMPTATIONS!
AND OTHER TIES

THE TIES
THAT BIND US

16.

SEX AND THE STAY-AT-HOME MOM

Being pregnant is a special time in a woman's life, and a truly romantic time for any couple. You kissed when the results were positive. You hugged when you heard the baby's heartbeat. You embraced when the nursery was completed. And you both wept when, after nine months, you finally agreed to doggy-style sex.

Yes, being pregnant is a glorious, romantic time. But actually having the baby is another story altogether. And it is usually at this time, the "transition" time to be exact, when the nature of your relationship may change. What am I talking about? Well, for those who haven't been there, I'm referring to that special moment between contractions when a woman grabs her husband by his Adam's apple, imbeds her longest nail, and hisses, "Touch me again and I'll cut it off, Jack!"

Of course, no woman in her right mind means it. You most certainly DO want to be touched again (just not right away). And you most certainly would never, ever "cut it off" (especially if you'd like to enlarge your brood). You've simply got other things on your mind, like a howling baby with chronic colic and a yowling mother-in-law who appears to suffer from the same malady. "Who's got time for sex?" you may find yourself muttering between burps, bottles, and yellow waxy buildup. "Who's got the energy for such a foolhardy activity—let alone the lingerie? Not me."

And so begins the sad saga of sex and the Stay-at-Home Mom, or any new mother for that matter. It's the age-old saga that places S-E-X on the back burner.

What's a mother to do? Well, the way I see it, you have two choices. You can do nothing and wonder why your husband's voice has changed. Or you can try a few of the techniques offered in my widely acclaimed "Seven Steps to Successful Sex for the Stay-at-Home Mom."

SEVEN STEPS TO SUCCESSFUL SEX
FOR THE STAY-AT-HOME MOM

1. Calorie-Laden Casseroles

Let's face it: It's only been a few months since your baby was born and you're not ready for sex yet. This would be hunky-dory except for that one hungry-eyed, sad-looking mug that stares at you morning, noon, and night, whimpering: "Haven't your stitches dissolved yet?"

Since you're bound to feel guilty, I strongly recommend that you feed your husband a heavy dose of casseroles at this point. Honestly, stuff him to the gills and I guarantee, after a while, he won't want sex either. This is purely an exercise in guilt reduction, and if I may say so myself, quite beautiful in its simplicity. As your interest picks up, though, be sure to cut back on the gloppy messes or you'll be making love to Orca.

2. Enticing Lingerie

I don't know about you, but I never bought all that so-called "maternity" lingerie. I intended to, but whenever I went to the store and saw the size of those gargantuan undies, I would bolt in horror. No, I simply wore what I owned, stretching the elastic to tension-defying lengths. And then, unbelievably, continued to wear it long after the baby was born, never thinking twice about the negative effect it was having on our sex life.

It wasn't until my husband said things like, "I'd snap the back of your big baggy bra but there's no elastic left," or "Do you really think those ratty pillowcases you call 'underwear' are a turn-on?" that it dawned on me to invest in some new lingerie. But I finally did; and I encourage you to do the same if you haven't already.

3. Sound Arousal

Remember that Pavlov's dog stuff from Psych. 101 where the dog salivated every time it heard the bell? Well, adapting the same technique to your life, I want you to visualize getting sexually aroused every time your baby cries. I know, I know, this seems impossible since the sound of a wailing infant makes us grow tense and rigid, clamping shut every orifice on our bodies tighter than a coffin.

But I urge you to give it a try and think, "Hot Sex, Hot Sex, Hot Sex" every time you hear, "Waaah, Waaah, Waaah." (Note: Consider skipping this step if your baby has chronic colic.)

4. Working Woman Attire

Forget about greeting your husband at the door decked only in Saran Wrap—that's too cold. And depending on how long it's been since you've given birth, it might make you look like a gigantic baked potato. Instead, greet him wearing the get-up of a Working Woman: suit, stockings, shellacked hair, pumps, and perfume. He'll take one look at you, think he's back in the office, and begin behaving towards you the way men and women typically behave in the office setting: flirting, winking, leering, pinching, and engaging in suggestive sexual banter. You two can go wild from here, creating all sorts of fantasies, such as, you're the boss and he's up for a raise, or he's the boss and you've just handed him a shoddy report, or you're both on your way to a cheesy convention in Dallas.

P.S. Leave out the fantasy where he's the boss and you're telling him you're pregnant. Bosses go limp whenever they hear that story.

5. Erotic Scents

Once a baby enters a home, all former smells are snuffed out by the ever-present, all-powerful Eau-de-Baby scent. And let me tell you, it's not a seductive aroma, unless, of course, you find raunchy diaper pails, crusty spittle, sour milk, and pungent little piggies sexually stimulating. My advice? Think "brothel" and alter the air molecules of your home accordingly with incense, aromatic candles, cheap perfume, whiskey-drenched throw pillows, and sweat.

6. TV Wildlife Specials

I know what you're thinking: Wildlife Specials? Get a life, honey! But hear me out. Ever rent an X-rated video to, uh, get the juices flowing? No, me neither. Too tawdry, too gross, too everybody in-the-store-knows-what-Miss-Muffet-is-up-to.

Enter TV Wildlife Specials. Ever watch them? Well, there's a little scenery, a little habitat stuff, and then hour after hour after hour of M-A-T-I-N-G—good, clean, more-positions-than-you-thought-possible mating. Give it a try.

7. Hormone Injections

If all else fails, you might want to think about getting a gallon-sized injection of estrogen. This should jump-start your sex drive as well as plump-up any dehydrated areas on your body.

Make sure it's estrogen and not testosterone, however, or you could wind up with a furry face, a hankering for Slim Jims, and a ferocious desire to purchase a "recliner."

17.

FRANK ANSWERS TO COMMON SEXUAL QUESTIONS

Q. Now that I'm a "mommy," I feel funny wearing provocative clothing. Will my desire for wearing, say, those really sleazy shirts with no shoulders ever return?

A. Hopefully, no.

Q. It's been so long since my husband and I have had sex, we've completely forgotten how. Now, what is it that we're supposed to do again?

A. Make sure you have some ice cubes handy and then go rent *9½ Weeks*. That should jog your memory. Or you could always try the zoo and see what the orangutans are up to.

Q. I've always been into "fantasy," but now when I close my eyes during sex, all I see is my trash collector who, by the way, is missing key front teeth. How can I get this unpleasant image out of my head?

A. Switch garbage companies. Maybe the next guy will be better looking.

Q. I feel so ashamed, I don't know where to begin. Three years ago, I became a Stay-at-Home Mom. Although I like being home (sort of), I must confess that since I no longer work, I feel subservient to my husband's every whim. I DO NOT LIKE THIS FEELING AT ALL. So you know what I did? I relied on the oldest trick in the book: I started to withhold sex to assert myself.

Sick, huh? Yeah, I thought so, too, until I saw that my withholding actually changed my husband's behavior, not to mention the way he walked. Once I tuned in to what was happening, I devised a crafty, result-dependent system of sexual rationing. Take a look.

If my husband:	*I withhold sex for*
Suggests I lose a few pounds	2 years
Talks nonstop about his fab secretary	1 year
Plays sinful amounts of golf	6 months
Feigns sleep when the baby is crying	5 months
Leaves mud on my newly waxed floor	4 months

Yells, "Who turned up the G.D. heat?"	3 months
Passes unbelievable amounts of gas	2 months
Won't listen to my meaningful dreams	1 month
Moans, "We never have sex anymore"	3 weeks
Asks why his underwear is pink	2 weeks

Now be honest. Am I a bad wife for relying on this ancient method of trying to control the living daylights out of my husband, especially in this day of applied feminism?

A.   It all depends. If, say, your husband comes home with as many as four naked women, then, yes, I guess you're a fool for shooing the big guy away. But more important, I think you need to search deeply within yourself and locate the answer to the more pressing question: Why is his underwear pink?

———

18.

ACCEPTABLE STAY-AT-HOME LIES

There, there, you've had a horrendous day, haven't you? Well, you're not alone. And you know what you do on really bad days? When confronted with yet another situation guaranteed to make your shoulders sag, you take a deep breath and LIE. It not only feels good, it puts you in control. To facilitate your lying and hone this all-important skill, I've provided a few "it's-okay-to-say" examples for your reading pleasure:

- When someone stops in unexpectedly and your house is a mess, it's okay to say:

    "The cleaning woman is coming tomorrow, so why bother?"

- When someone asks if you're pregnant and you're not, it's okay to say:

  "Yes."

- When a charity calls and asks you to solicit door to door, it's okay to say:

  "I'm just the babysitter; you'll have to call back."

- When someone comments on how huge your baby is, it's okay to say:

  "That big thing? That's not mine, that's my sister's."

- When a Working Mom asks if you could watch her sick child, it's okay to say:

  "Sorry, I'm flat out with the flu, too."

- When you look like a complete slob and happen to run into an old friend, it's okay to say:

  "I'm on my way to the gym, ta-ta."

- When someone says they saw you slamming down beers at the local hangout, it's okay to say:

  "I have a twin."

- When your mother-in-law calls and asks if she could swing by to see the baby, it's okay to say:

  "We're on our way out."

- When your mother-in-law stops by anyway and pounds on the door with the force of a killer hurricane, all the while screaming, "I know you're in there; now let me in," it's okay to say:

  "Sorry, we all have strep."

- When your shopping cart is loaded with Fruity Pebbles, Gummi Bears, Skittles, Teddy Grahams, Cheez Whiz, and Pop-Tarts, and you happen to encounter the most health-conscious mom you know, it's okay to say:

  > "I'm shopping for my neighbor who's in the hospital. Think she eats enough junk food or what!"

- When someone calls and asks what all the racket is in the background, it's okay to say:

  > "It's the workmen next door."

- When your husband calls, hears the TV, and asks what you're watching, it's okay to say:

  > "Gee, I don't know. I'm right in the middle of reviewing multiplication tables with the baby."

- When someone you don't really care about asks if your baby has rolled over yet (and she hasn't), it's okay to say:

  > "Rolled over and did a triple somersault right out of her crib."

19.

STAY-AT-HOME GUILT

We all know what we *should* be doing, but sometimes it's not as easy as others think. So here are the "shoulds" we strive for because, well, we're home all day, and you know, it's expected. These "shoulds" are followed by the "realities" that induce guilt because, well, we're home all day, AND YOU KNOW HOW IT GETS.

We *should* have stellar kids.

> Kids are kids and they all get away with some degree of murder—okay, a big degree of murder—oh, all right, they call the shots!

We *should* have tidy homes.

> Why bother anymore? The desire for chaos reigns supreme among the young and the restless.

We *should* fix really nutritious meals.

> We did up until that regrettable moment our kids discovered the 5th food group: SUGAR.

We *should* nix TV watching.

> Ever try playing peek-a-boo at the crack of dawn? It's humanly impossible.

We *should* wake up happy.

> The urge to complain wells inside us like a weed that won't die. We're victims, really.

We *should* organize neighborhood block parties.

> Right. We have nothing better to do than bring a bunch of people together who probably don't even like each other.

We *should* have drapes on all our windows.

> Yeah, and our stereo speakers shouldn't serve as end tables. Who's got the time to decorate?

We *should* read the paper every day.

> If only devouring Ann Landers and our horoscopes counted . . .

We *should* go outside with the kids every day.

> You mean, plunking the kid in the sandbox while we watch from the window doesn't count?

We *should* care about our appearance.

> What's the point of dressing up when (1) we can toss on the same smelly sweats we've been wearing for weeks; and (2) no one's coming over?

We *should* volunteer.

> It's just so darn hard to help someone else when we can barely find our keys each day.

We *should* have the in-laws over at least once a month.

> No can do. Any more faces to feed on a regular basis will cause us to commit a crime.

We *should* have completed "baby books."

> Isn't sacrificing our souls by staying home enough doting to last a lifetime? Must we chronicle every burp, too?

We *should* remain abreast of top parenting techniques.

> Yes, we should. But we always seem to choose *People* over *Parents* when confronted with that one minute of free time.

20.

TOP TEN STAY-AT-HOME TEMPTATIONS TO AVOID

1. Pulling the shades, switching on the TV, and watching soap after soap after soap.

2. Calling your husband at work every 15 minutes with a stool-color update.

3. Dressing your children better than you dress yourself.

4. Asking the child of a Working Woman, "You miss mommy-poo, don't you?"

5. Cleaning the grout on a daily basis with Clorox and a toothbrush.

6. Grazing at the pantry from sunup to sundown.

7. Scheduling the plumber for Monday, the painter for Tuesday, the electrician for Wednesday . . . anything for a little company!

8. Snatching the baby from your husband and sniping, "Oh, here. Let ME do it!"

9. Proudly showing *anyone* who stops in the up-close-and-personal videotape your husband took the night Junior was born.

10. Welcoming a door-to-door religious fanatic with open arms and a slice of *küchen*.

21.

CORRUPTION IN THE KITCHEN

When people ask me what I do, I usually say, "I'm *home* raising my kids." But you know what I should really say— "I'm *in the kitchen* raising my kids."

The kitchen. Morning, noon, and night: the kitchen. I'm always in the kitchen. We are always in the kitchen. We live in the kitchen. The kitchen and I are one.

And you know what's happened? I've become a derelict in my own kitchen—a corrupt cook. I kick Cheerios under the fridge because I'm too lazy to pick them up. I guzzle Hawaiian Punch straight from the can. And I even (gasp) microwave formula and baby food.

I haven't always been such a shameful chef. Not too long ago, when I was carefree and spending much less time in the old crumb castle, I was better about meeting health-code requirements.

But not anymore. No, I've loosened my apron strings about as far as they'll go in my search for lower, more livable standards. And it feels good—truly liberating and strangely powerful.

After you've spent a couple of years imprisoned in your kitchen, you too may notice that your standards have dropped. No cause for worry. It's only natural given your new round-the-clock priorities. Come to think of it, it's not only natural, it's a good sign—a true indication you've progressed beyond thinking that a kitchen devoid of bacteria is actually something to pursue. (See Chapter 22: Maslow's Hierarchy of Needs for complete affirmation of your kitchen misconduct.)

How corrupt are you in the kitchen? If you're not afraid to find out, take the following test.

KITCHEN CORRUPTION QUIZ

Have you ever:	Yes	No
1. Served food that has dropped on the floor?	——	——
2. Thought "salmonella" was the name of a female fish?	——	——
3. Sneezed on food and served it anyway?	——	——
4. Cleaned utensils with "spit?"	——	——

		Yes	No
5.	Used food way, way, way past its expiration date?	___	___
6.	Moved the fridge and found enough food for a caserole underneath?	___	___
7.	Owned flour that . . . moves?	___	___
8.	Opened your fridge and fainted from the putrid odor?	___	___
9.	Claimed credit for cooking something "store bought?"	___	___
10.	Wondered why there are so many moths in your pantry?	___	___
11.	Licked beaters and then promptly used them again—without washing?	___	___
12.	Discovered the remnants of nocturnal creatures in your pans?	___	___
13.	Guzzled a beverage straight from the carton?	___	___
14.	Served Rice Krispies for dinner?	___	___
15.	Gone years without cleaning your oven?	___	___

Telltale Bonus Question: (Add 100 points for this one!)

| 16. | Had sex anywhere near the kitchen sink? | ___ | ___ |

SCORING:

For each "Yes," give yourself 1 point. No points for "No." Don't forget to add 100 points if you answered "Yes" to the Telltale Bonus Question.

0-2   Have you ever considered becoming an inspector for the FDA?

3-6   Lighten up, June. Germs build a child's immunity, you know. Besides, a little mommy misconduct now and then is good for the soul.

7-10   You're almost there. Commit a few more "little naughties" and you'll be ruling the roost in no time.

11-15   Bravo! Give yourself a big pat on the back. You've gone perfectly astray without going repulsively overboard.

100+   And to think you were actually surprised when *Better Homes and Gardens* rejected the recipe you submitted to their "Prize Tested Recipes Contest."

22.

MASLOW'S HIERARCHY OF NEEDS

TRADITIONAL

Self-Actualization
Self-Esteem
Belonging
Safety
Psychological Needs

NEW & IMPROVED VERSION FOR THE STAY-AT-HOME MOM

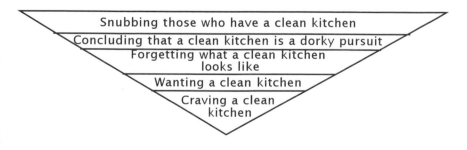

Snubbing those who have a clean kitchen
Concluding that a clean kitchen is a dorky pursuit
Forgetting what a clean kitchen looks like
Wanting a clean kitchen
Craving a clean kitchen

PART 5

THE CHARACTERS WHO
RUFFLE OUR FEATHERS.

SIGNIFICANT
OTHERS

23.

THE OTHER WOMAN . . .

You are introduced to her in a most unsuspecting manner. Perhaps over a ham dinner. Perhaps after you've just stepped out of the shower. You see your husband shake his head, close his eyes, and grin. "Whaaaat?" you say, grinning yourself.

Contrary to what you're expecting him to say, like, "Wow! You look more beautiful today than the day we married," he simply says, "She is a *Godsend*."

"Who?" you ask incredulously, your insecurities bubbling to the surface.

"Why, Deborah, my fabulous new assistant," he says without a hitch. "The girl I was telling you about last night when you were bending over pulling on your Tweetie Bird pajamas. The one with the Swedish accent and the tiny mole on her upper lip.

"Oh, Deborah, not her again," you think.

But before you can say, "Put a lid on it, you big nincompoop," your husband is off and running with his Deborah-does-this and Deborah-does-that stories.

Giggling like a pimply teenager and looking as smitten as Peppy La Pew, he tells you about the cute way she thinks "irregardless" is a word. (Ha!) He mentions the silly time she acknowledged his birthday by sending a belly dancer to his office. (What a charmer.) And he rattles on and on about her knockout coffee, her super-duper filing system, and her contagious, upbeat office spirit. (Stop, please!)

Though you know he's not having anything as stupid as an affair—he's married to YOU, after all—you find that you can't help but wonder about their daily tête-à-têtes. Do they laugh? Do they compliment each other? Do they ever discuss . . . you?

It gets to be too much.

And so one morning, after spending a restless night plotting Deborah's premature demise, you nonchalantly ask, "Tell me, do you and Deborah ever go to lunch?"

"Occasionally," he says, nonplused. "But not much lately. She's in the hospital, having a fibroid tumor removed from her left fallopian tube."

"Uh, excuse me?" you snap, absolutely floored by the depth of knowledge your beloved possesses about this, this other woman's interior!

"It's benign—nothing to worry about," he says, "Guess she's having that mole removed, too. Apparently it's been a great source of pain and insecurity for her."

"Ah yes, the one that makes her look like Cindy Crawford," you snort. "Gee, I can almost feel her pain."

"Yeah, that one," he says, oblivious to your mounting fury. "And since we're on the subject, do you think you could send her some flowers?"

"Don't think so," you say as you position a chair leg in the middle of his bare foot and sit down with a vengeance. "Don't think so at all."

Maybe a fabulous assistant and all of her cunning, annoying ways will never intersect your life. But for lots of moms, this woman can be an esteem-zapping nightmare. As one mom put it, "Not only does she do all the things I don't have time to do anymore, like, you know, straighten his crooked lapel and laugh at his lame jokes, but she does them in a dress. How can you beat that?"

Well, moms, the good news is: You can beat it. First though, you need to take your husband aside, put his head in a squeeze-lock, and demand that he never breathe her name in your presence again. Having done that, take a good look at Chapter 24, "How to Reduce a Fabulous Assistant to Rubble," for guaranteed ways to knock the wind right out of her puffy little sails and remind her who's QUEEN OF THE HILL.

24.

HOW TO REDUCE A FABULOUS ASSISTANT TO RUBBLE

- Never forget to mispronounce her name, each and every time you see her.

- Never forget to give her a life-sized Smurf for Secretary's Day.

- Never forget to say, "Gosh, you can practically feel the cells spreading every time you sit down, can't you?"

- Never forget to say, "Now that's what I call an <u>interesting</u> haircut."

- Never forget to treat her like a small child by patting her on the head.

- Never forget to press the "delete" key on her computer when she's not looking.

- Never forget to say, "I heard the office will be downsizing soon . . ."

- Never forget to correct her pronunciation and grammar.

- Never forget to say, "My husband has a raging case of jock itch. Think you could pick him up some Cruex on your lunch hour?"

- Never forget to wrinkle your nose and say, "What's burning?" when you pass by the coffee room.

25.

THE OTHER MAN . . .

Three months have gone by, and except for your husband, your mother, and the cashier at the grocery store, you haven't communicated with another adult since your baby was born. The harsh reality of staying home and losing touch with the human race is beginning to settle in. And you don't like it.

"How do Eskimo moms do it?" you wonder. "How the heck do they endure such long, lonely days and not go completely nuts? How can they stand the cold? How do they decorate their igloos anyway? And, and . . ."

Your mind is spinning like a roulette wheel when the doorbell rings. Ah yes, the repairman. He's come to fix the disposal and you don't want to keep him waiting. He's human after all, and considering your lack of contact with the species, you're curious to see if it's evolved.

Once settled, you drag a chair over to where he's working and study him with intense fascination. "What's that for?"

"It's a wrench, ma'am, and it'll help me loosen that bolt there, that is, if you'll ease your chair out of the way and let me under the sink."

You move your chair a fraction of an inch back and continue to monitor his every move. Despite the fact that the amount of hair covering his body would put a gorilla to shame, you feel renewed fondness for all of mankind. You find yourself smiling, and edge your chair back to where it was.

"My leg, ma'am. The chair is on my leg."

"Oh, sorry 'bout that," you reply, thinking how friendly he seems, perhaps the kindest man you've ever met in your entire life (excluding your husband, of course). An appreciative tear wells in your happy eye.

On a lark, you decide to tell him how incredibly grateful you are that he is the one fixing your drain.

You take a deep and meaningful breath. You straighten your shoulders. But just as you're about to share your heart and soul with him, he does the unthinkable.

He leans forward. He grunts. He yanks a tool from his tool belt. And then he does it. He exposes the . . . the . . . the crack of the century!

"OMIGOD," you scream, running willy-nilly out of the room, arms flailing, hair flying, tears springing.

"Ma'am?" he calls. "Somethin' wrong?"

Once in the safety of your bedroom, you grab your husband's picture and smother it with kisses, feeling relieved, confused, embarrassed, and nauseous. "What was I thinking?" you ask the mirror. "Opening up my heart to a complete stranger! W-w-what's happening to me?"

A repairman plays a curious role in the Stay-at-Home Mom's life. Depending on the depths of your domestic despair, you may find yourself actually looking forward to his arrival. Worse, you may find yourself engaging in uncharacteristic behavior like putting on lipstick before he arrives, feigning interest in the work he's doing, or asking his opinion about—of all things—potty training. Or you may even find yourself (ugh!) wondering if he thinks you are interesting or attractive.

Should you be concerned? Not really. You're human, after all, and humans have been known to behave strangely when they've felt pent up for long periods of time.

But if, say, you don't run for cover when the big guy bends over, then I suggest you consult "Every Mother's Guide to Repairman Etiquette" and memorize the rules ASAP.

26.

EVERY MOTHER'S GUIDE TO REPAIRMAN ETIQUETTE

TIME-TESTED RULES

- Never answer the door in your loosely clasped bathrobe.

- Never say these words: "I had the most unusual dream about you last night . . ."

- Never offer champagne as the refreshing beverage.

- Never ask him to feel your leg to determine if your shaver is dull.

- Never have saxophone music playing softly in the background.

- Never ask him to zip up the skin-tight dress you shouldn't be wearing in the first place.

- Never accidentally-on-purpose lose your balance as you bend down to inspect his work.

- Never start singing, "What's love got to do, got to do with it . . ."

- Never offer to press his uniform.

- Never comment on his skillful, rugged hands and then ask to read his palms.

- Never throw yourself at his feet, sobbing, "I've never been so lonely in all my life!"

27.

SPECIAL REPAIRMAN TIP

Never say, "Sure, I understand," when the repairman is (1) over an hour late or (2) has failed to call to advise you that he's running late. Below are three handy ways to deal with this frustrating, albeit common, tardy-o scenario. Choose the one that best suits your personality:

- Slam the door in his face, hopefully catching his tardy nose as you do.

- Allow him to come in, but blast him from ear to shining ear in your shrillest voice.

- Leave a note on the door: "Had to go out. Watch out for 'Shredder,' our German Shepherd. He has a thing for sweat and overalls."

28.

THE NUDGE...

Her watchful face is clenched in a disapproving scowl. "NOW why is the baby crying?" she barks, stomping her perturbed foot. You've been hearing this exasperating comment for days, ever since you brought your little butterball home from the hospital, and you're ready to throttle the source.

"My babies never cried like that. Never!" she huffs

You follow her movements with predator eyes, the eyes of a Great White. The word "strangle" consumes every living cell of your weary body.

"Swaddle tighter, dear. Oh my goodness, not like that. Like THIS."

You bite your tongue. Ten yards of stitches you-know-where and a hemorrhoid ring the size of a Michelin tire give new meaning to the words "sit tight."

Unable to move and too tired to object, you watch this other woman slowly but surely become a permanent fixture in your home, tidying up here and rearranging there. The week "just to help out" has turned to two, and you're wondering when this other woman, also known as the mother-in-law, secretly called The Nudge, will hightail it out of your home.

"My babies never had all that acne," she states one day. "Something's definitely wrong."

"She's purging my, my, my excess hormones!" you wail at the top of your lungs, breaking again the millions of facial capillaries that broke during that extra-special moment when your doctor urged you to push harder.

Just then your husband walks in. "Soooo, how are the two moms hitting it off?"

Both of you look away. Neither of you respond.

Let's face it, most mothers-in-law behave quite differently once a grandchild is involved. Content to ignore you in the past, now they're all over the place like flies on fruit. And they won't go away.

(If I may diverge for just a moment, I would like to say that not all mothers-in-law tweak and irritate their daughters-in-law. One really sweet one was found lurking around that big mall in Minnesota. Lots of sweet ones are living it up overseas. And, of course, there's my own mother-in-law who, if it were not for the big knitting needle aimed at my temple as I write these words, would be considered quite lovely herself.)

Most mothers-in-law, though, have a sixth sense for making their son's wife absolutely, positively, undeniably miserable. Which is why it's best to nip things in the bud, before, you know, a contractor shows up one day with estimates for an "in-law addition," and you suddenly find yourself under her Olds . . . rigging the breaks.

One surefire way to deal with an overzealous mother-in-law is to ask her if she could watch the baby for a week while you and your husband ride the wild Hawaiian surf. If she agrees, you probably won't see her for quite some time. Hey, she's no glutton for punishment. And if she doesn't agree, you won't see her hanging around either. She'll be too afraid you might ask again. So no matter how you look at it, it's a win-win situation.

For more tips on how to maintain the upper hand in your relationship with your beloved's mother, check out Chapter 29 — How to Manage a Meddling Mother-in-Law. Practice a few of these and you might not see her until the kids start college!

29.

HOW TO MANAGE A MEDDLING MOTHER-IN-LAW

Never ask your mother-in-law her opinion on anything. And never, ever, forget to . . .

1. Remind her that parenting techniques have evolved beyond remarks such as, "God is watching."

2. Hand her your baby when its diaper is LOADED.

3. Send her your sky-high dentist bill with a note saying: "Thanks a million for all the Gummi Bears. Really, you're a peach."

4.   Set out all of your cleaning supplies before she arrives.

5.   Serve really bad coffee and stale Stella Doros.

6.   Bring up some of her son's peculiar habits with a hint of suspicion, blame, and reproach in your voice.

7.   Thank her over and over for calling during your baby's nap.

8.   Go deaf and hum to yourself when she asks why your baby isn't rolling over yet.

9.   Perk up and give her a big hug on her way out.

30.

WMN:
THE WORKING-MOTHER
NEIGHBOR

O h, look. Look! There she is. The Working-Mother Neighbor. And there she goes. Zoooooom! Off to work in the "real" world.

You were just about to sneak out to get the morning paper in your ratty flannels when you spotted her. Slinking ever so quickly out of sight, you observed her brisk walk, her crisp suit, her coiffed hair.

Seeing her—or for that matter, any Working Woman—triggers an indescribable feeling. Is it envy? Nah, you conquered that a long time ago. Anger? Nah, her insensitive remarks don't bug you anymore. Sympathy? A little; she must miss her kids. Irritation?

Maybe a little of that too; she does always seem more interested in what hubby has to say.

What about curiosity? Yeah! That's it. Curiosity! And you know the feeling is mutual. You wonder how the heck she can abandon her darling cherubs, while at the same time, she wonders how the heck you can endure a life she finds as stimulating as watching toenails grow.

When the coast is clear, you scurry down to get the paper. But wait! What's that? Oh, no. Here comes another Working Mother Neighbor. She's on a power walk of all things, splitting atoms with each swing of her superior arm.

It's too late to turn back, so you muster all the dignity you have and wave a brave "hello." She nods her head, gives you a rapid once-over—settling on your tattered sleeves—and smiles the most peculiar smile.

Where have you seen that smile? Ah, yes. Now you remember. It's the same smile your mother gave you when you told her you wanted to learn how to fly a stunt plane. A pathetic you-don't-really-expect-me-to-take-you-seriously kind of smile.

You trudge back in, feeling drained of self-esteem. What is it about Working Mothers that makes you feel so sheepish, so dowdy, so Donna Reed-ish?

You ponder the answer while unloading the dishwasher and decide that most Working Mothers sincerely don't respect the nature of your work. Oh sure, they might pretend they do. But you know otherwise, thanks to their endless supply of curious little remarks—remarks like, "I could never do what you're doing. I'd die from the boredom. I'd just die!"

Who *are* these Working-Mother Neighbors (WMN)? And why do they raise our dander so?

Compiling years of keen observations, I've concluded that she—the annoying she, that is—comes in one of three forms:

- the Witness-Protection-Program WMN

- the Need-a-Favor WMN

- the Let's-Be-Friends (not) WMN

The one other Working Mother Neighbor, the Terrific WMN, *does* exist. And I'm happy to report that she sincerely respects our at-home efforts. But to be perfectly honest, she's no fun to write about. The other ones are though! So read on . . .

THE WITNESS-PROTECTION-PROGRAM WMN

Is she alive? Who knows anymore. You haven't seen her for days, let alone months.

Double-strength blinds shroud her front windows. Huge pines camouflage what may be the front door. A massive garage door remains hermetically sealed. And, with the exception of that millisecond when she tossed Halloween candy from a distance of eight feet, you've never even seen the inside of her house.

She's the most peculiar Working Mother Neighbor. Here she's lived next door for years, and you know little about her other than she's married, she works, and she might have one or two kids. Would you recognize her? Of course not! How could you recognize someone who never strolls out to collect her mail, but rather extracts it with reptilian agility from the tinted window of her car?

Though you have no relationship with her, you can't help but feel slightly irritated by her presence. Why did she move to a neighborhood of all places when she has so little interest in neighborly living? What is she running from anyway?

How can she justify keeping her kids indoors so much? And who does she think she is not thanking you for the rum balls you so generously placed on her doorstep last December?

One night you suggest to your husband that it would be a good idea to get to know the neighbors better, perhaps invite them over some Sunday for a cookout. His confused, vacant look followed by a plaintive "why?" confirms your original decision to keep your distance.

And so it goes. You. The Witness-Protection-Program Working Mother. And your sporadic intrigue with her clandestine (presumably corrupt) life.

Tip for Getting Along:

> *Do nothing; expect nothing; feel nothing. But do invest in a decent pair of binoculars.*

THE NEED-A-FAVOR WMN

She's the first to notice you've lost weight, the first to compliment your new haircut, and the first to acknowledge what a good mother you are. But aside from being a full-time "favor provider" for this Working Mother Neighbor, your relationship isn't worth a bean.

Oh sure, you're friendly with each other and can share a hoot now and again. But the truth is, you resent her nonstop, belittling requests to do this and take care of that and pick up this and drop off that. The favors, seemingly small and always referred to as "quick," are asked under the incorrect assumption that because you're home all day, well by golly, you must have all the free-e-e-e-e time in the world. How wrong this Working Mother Neighbor is!

One day she goes too far though. One day she asks the MOTHER of all favors. She asks if you could watch her unruly kids for just a little while after school until she comes home from work. And she wonders if you could do it for "just a little half-year."

The request blows your stay-at-home doors off. You toy with grabbing her by the lapel and screaming: "Not! In! Your! Lifetime! Lady!" But instead, you collect your senses, remember that your kids play with her kids, and calmly say, "I'm not home at that time of day."

She cocks an eyebrow: She knows you're home then. You cock an eyebrow back: Of course you're home then. But neither of you say another word.

And she never asks you for another favor? Only in your dreams! Give her a week and she'll be back begging for more. Or at least, giving it a try.

Tip for Getting Along:

> *Never jump on the "favor-train" in the first place.*

THE LET'S BE FRIENDS (NOT) WMN

Of the three, the Let's-Be-Friends (not) Working Mother Neighbor will confuse and frustrate you the most. Here's why: One minute she's dying to be your good friend, and the next, she she can't remember your name.

The relationship unfolds something like this: You meet one Saturday while strolling your kids and you hit it off immediately. You like the same clothes, books, music, etc., and even have the same difficulties with your kids.

Conversation flows, punctuated by lots of laughs and future plans to get together. Filled with excitement, you rush home and tell your husband all about your great, new, funny friend. "The problem is, though," you hear yourself lamenting, "she works."

And in no time, you soon discover that this problem is downright monumental. A night out you've looked forward to for weeks is quickly canceled when your good friend's meeting runs late. A Saturday shopping trip is kiboshed seconds before departure when your good friend feels too tired to go. Your child's birthday party is innocently forgotten by your harried, working good friend.

Time marches on without a peep from your good friend. And you sadly resign yourself to the cruel fact that she has no time for you, that friends just aren't as important to her.

Then, months down the road, when you least expect it, your now-forgotten friend calls to see if you want to join her on a power walk. Your head says "no," your heart says "go."

What do you do? You go, knowing that for a very brief period of exceptionally shallow, wildly insincere time you have an imitation good friend.

Tip for Getting Along:

> *Give what you get, and cancel occasionally to maintain your self-respect. When you do cancel, always do it at the very last minute.*

PART 6

HARD TO FIND BUT EASY TO BEFRIEND
(SUPERMOMS EXCLUDED)

OTHER
STAY-AT-HOME
MOTHERS

31.

WHERE IS EVERYBODY?

*L*ike many Stay-at-Home Moms, you probably worked until the day you had your first contraction. You probably had an exciting coterie of working friends you were sorry to leave behind. And you probably were quite surprised when contact with them dwindled, dwindled, dwindled, and then—poof!—dried up altogether. I know I was.

Even if you didn't work, things changed between friends, didn't they? Single friends stopped coming around as much. "Whaddayamean you're out of beer?" And friends without kids could only stand the constant crying so long. "I didn't think babies could cry that loud." Why, even friends *with* kids quit calling. "My kids need playmates their own age."

And then it finally happens. You wake up one day without a real friend in the world. "I have no friends," you say to your bald little baby. "I guess mommy better dust off her friendship-making skills and go make some new ones. I don't see a problem with that, do you?"

But then you discover that indeed there is a problem—a big problem. Other Stay-at-Home Moms are hard to find. And finding one that might be your partner in crime is darn near impossible.

Full of hope, you scour your neighborhood first. You stroll your baby ever so slowly by those homes with the garage door up and the Little Tikes toys strewn haphazardly across the lawn.

"Where is everybody?" you wonder.

Undeterred, you plow on to the next cul-de-sac. There, a fit, perky woman in her forties—a Soccer Mom, no doubt—walks briskly toward you. "Three months?" she asks, peering into the stroller. "How did you know?" you reply, blinded by her happy smile.

"Believe me, I know," she says with the wisdom of a woman who's been there and back. "But now, tee hee, they're both in school."

As you watch her waltz away, presumably to a glorious life full of uninterrupted sleep and matching socks, you think morosely to yourself, "I will never get to that point. I just know it."

With "neighborhoods" crossed off your list, you head for the nearest Romp-'n-Run Gym for Kids. Expecting to chat, what a surprise it is to find yourself so tired from following your kid around the back-breaking obstacle course, you collapse, lifeless and speechless, in the nearest corner. That, combined with Rompo, the smelly germ-laden clown kids were forced to kiss, soon makes Romp-'n-Run a no-go as well.

Fortunately, a "Rec" center pamphlet arrives on your 265th day of captivity, and you sign up for a "Music with Mommy" class. Contact is made with other Stay-at-Home Moms, and gradually, ever so gradually, you compile an assortment of terrific friends who meet a variety of needs: the call-in-a-pinch mom, the best-advice-ever mom, the could-be-a-doctor mom, the best-bargains-around mom, the guzzle-a-beer mom, the great-recipes mom, and so on.

"Friends, at last," you sigh. "My life feels whole again."

So you see, moms, friendships do occur. It may take a couple of years and a few hundred Excedrin (to help you endure those endless days alone with the cubs), but eventually you'll meet moms you like.

32.

HOW TO MAKE FRIENDS FASTER

But maybe you don't want to wait a couple of years. Or maybe you're having a tough time making new friends because you keep making friends with the wrong kind of mom—a mom who has absolutely nothing in common with you save for the fact that you both . . . reproduced.

What should you do? I suggest you take a look at the profiles I've compiled for the seven most common Stay-at-Home Moms. You'll notice they've been designed to give you the goods on someone from the get-go. (Put another way: My insights significantly reduce the odds of finding out the friend you've pinned high hopes on turns out to be a lemon—to you, that is. She could be an absolute peach of a friend for someone else.)

Here's how to use the profiles. Next time you meet a mom with friendship potential, recall some of the key characteristics outlined in my profiles, NOTICE HER SHOES, ask a few unobtrusive questions like, "Er, uh, what's your favorite magazine?" and then see which profile she matches most closely. If it's near enough to the kind of mom you are, *voil*à, you're on your way to making a new friend.

(Note: I made a point of placing *"notice her shoes"* in caps because, quite frankly, shoes—not eyes—are the mirrors of the soul. So if you completely forget the profiles, worry not. You can usually tell a lot about someone just by observing what kind of shoes they wear. And for men, of course, it's the shoe size that reveals, well, you know. Ha, ha. Not really; it's the size of his nose!)

TELLTALE SIGNS OF A PRINCESS MOM

Former Profession: Any job that put her in a position to marry well.

Shoes: Shiny alligator pumps with a stacked heel.

Hairstyle: A fluffy yet windproof, permed concoction.

Daily Outfit: Skintight leather pants, cashmere sweater, oodles of gold jewelry.

Nails: Red fake things that go rat-a-tat-tat.

Fantasy Repairman: Fabio.

Parenting Tip: Boarding school from infancy on.

Cleaning Tip: Leave when the help arrives.

Breast-Feeding Tip: Ha!

Favorite Magazine: *Town and Country.*

Favorite Hors d' oeuvre: Stuffed grape leaves prepared by Carmen, the cook.

TELLTALE SIGNS OF AN OLD-FASHIONED MOM

Former Profession: Never worked.

Shoes: Lace-up tan Hush Puppies with arch supports.

Hairstyle: Short and painstakingly curled with bristle rollers.

Daily Outfit: Corduroy skirt; plaid shirt with darts, an apron during meal preparation.

Nails: Round little half-moons frosted pink.

Fantasy Repairman: Pat Roberts.

Parenting Tip: If in doubt, look to Miss Manners for guidance.

Cleaning Tip: There's nothing like a little "elbow grease" to get the job done.

Breast-Feeding Tip: Be sure to chafe your nipples red 'n raw with a rough washcloth to prepare them for feeding. To make a rough washcloth: Spread Elmer's Glue all over a washcloth; then sprinkle huge wood chips on it.

Favorite Magazine: *Good Housekeeping* from the '50s.

Favorite Hors d' oeuvre: Deviled eggs.

TELLTALE SIGNS OF A GO-GET-'EM MOM

Former Profession: Gym teacher/convention coordinator/real estate agent (or any job that demanded boundless energy and a round-the-clock smile).

Shoes: Sneakers, what else?

Hairstyle: A short, snappy do that looks as good wet as it does dry.

Daily Outfit: A perky tri-colored jogging or sweat set.

Nails: Neat, short, natural.

Fantasy Repairman: Tom Cruise.

Parenting Tip: A little soap in the mouth never hurt anyone.

Cleaning Tip: Set aside Monday to clean; and stick to it, gals.

Breast-Feeding Tip: Express it, freeze, use for soup base.

Favorite Magazine: *Parents.*

Favorite Hors d' oeuvre: Baked artichoke dip: It's fast, inexpensive, always a crowd-pleaser.

TELLTALE SIGNS OF A YUPPIE MOM

Former Profession: Art director, clothing designer, media buyer; or any job that had a cappuccino maker on the premises.

Shoes: Black cowboy boots or clogs.

Hairstyle: Blunt, trendy, carefree with highlights and lowlights.

Daily Outfit: Gap jeans, Eddie Bauer belt, Banana Republic T-shirt, J. Crew workshirt, Calvin Klein underwear.

Nails: Squared "french" nails with clear gloss.

Fantasy Repairman: Sam Sheppard.

Parenting Tip: Never, ever miss your weekly "night out" with the gals.

Cleaning Tip: Hire help if you can afford it; if not, lower your expectations.

Breast-Feeding Tip: When the going gets tough, the tough supplement with formula.

Favorite Magazine: *New Yorker.*

Favorite Hors d' oeuvre: Bruschetta with sundried tomatoes, brine-cured olives, and Montrachet cheese.

TELLTALE SIGNS OF AN EX-HIPPIE EARTH MOM

Former Profession: Cook in a vegetarian restaurant, weaver, potter, social worker; or any job that was spiritually satisfying.

Shoes: Birkenstocks, even in the winter.

Hairstyle: Long, pulled back in a loose braid, perhaps prematurely gray.

Daily Outfit: Gauze skirt or baggy pants with an over-sized Peruvian top.

Nails: A bit ragged from hauling crates at the co-op store.

Fantasy Repairman/men: Ben *and* Jerry.

Parenting Tip: A big communal bed creates confident, secure kids.

Cleaning Tip: A little vinegar goes a long way.

Breast-Feeding Tip: A full set of teeth doesn't hurt that much!

Favorite Magazine: *Vegetarian Times.*

Favorite Hors d' oeuvre: Garlicky humus with pita bread.

TELLTALE SIGNS OF A WILD MOM

Former Profession: Any job that allowed her to stand upright and strut her stuff.

Shoes: Backless anything with heels.

Hairstyle: Long and permed with sky-high bangs.

Daily Outfit: Cutoffs, tank top, belly ring, ankle bracelet.

Nails: Long, two-toned nails with imbedded stones.

Fantasy Repairman: Tommy Lee.

Parenting Tip: Round-the-clock TV never hurt anyone.

Cleaning Tip: If it doesn't stink, why bother?

Breast-Feeding Tip: The darker the beer the better.

Favorite Magazine: *National Enquirer.*

Favorite Hors d' oeuvre: Nachos with Cheez Whiz.

TELLTALE SIGNS OF A TYPICAL MOM

Former Profession: Did something, but can't recall exactly what it was.

Shoes: Anything without laces, or whatever is closest to the door.

Hairstyle: Chin-length with a headband.

Daily Outfit: Black leggings/sweats with a giant T-shirt that reads: "If Mama Ain't Happy, Ain't Nobody Happy."

Nails: What nails?

Fantasy Repairman: The current repairman.

Parenting Tip: Make sure your bathrooms have deadbolts.

Cleaning Tip: Gather up toys, open the basement door, throw them all downstairs, close the door.

Breast-Feeding Tip: Stay away from beans!

Favorite Magazine: *People.*

Favorite Hors d' oeuvre: Anything prepared in a restaurant.

33.

THE SUPERMOM

Sooner or later you'll meet HER. And you'll know she's a *you-know* because of her home, her exquisitely neat, every-room-stenciled, smells-like-fresh-bread home.

You'll comment on her gorgeous love seat. "That old thing?" she'll say. "I reupholstered it with my feet while I was breast-feeding Megan."

You'll notice her lush, cascading drapes. "Those?" she'll say. "I whipped them up while I was recovering from hand surgery."

You'll remark that her son actually ate his spinach. "What nutritionally aware child wouldn't?" she'll say. "Why, it's absolutely bursting with fiber and Vitamin A."

And you'll never, ever, ever want to be her friend.

I knew a Supermom once. We were acquainted for about a week, but then I couldn't take the pain anymore and stopped going over to her house. Pain? you ask. Yes; big, palpable pain. Sure, I'd bring it on myself by the comparisons I'd invariably make after we'd been together, but I couldn't help it. I'd see her spectacular furniture, go home, look at the crates holding my stereo, and collapse in a twitching heap on the floor. Or I'd catch a glimpse of her immaculate garage, recall my own disgusting garage—an area so loaded with junk we couldn't park our cars in it if we wanted to—and buckle over from jealous cramps. It was too much.

Luckily, I was able to extract myself from her pristine paws quite easily. But maybe you're in a situation where it's impossible not to have contact with a Supermom.

Perhaps she's in your playgroup or the only mom for miles around or so generous with hand-me-downs you don't want to give her the big chill. If that's the case, then you'll need to find ways to accommodate Mother Superior without letting her turn your innards inside out.

34.

HOW TO CLIP A SUPERMOM'S WINGS

IMPORTANT NE'ER-DOs

- Never ask her how she keeps so annoyingly thin.

- Never forget to sneak out of the grocery store before Ms. High-'n-Mighty begins to conduct a nutritional analysis of your sorry cart.

- Never fail to ignore the hundreds of kiddie sports trophies that decorate her shelves.

- Never forget to sniff the air and say, "Have you had your house checked for carbon monoxide leaks?"

- Never forget to clench your jaw tighter than a steel drum whenever you feel the urge to compliment her.

- Never mention the gazillion cavities already propagating in your little one's mouth.

- Never ask: "Do you have a degree in interior decorating?"

- Never point out that her exceptionally well-dressed, well-behaved children never seem to fight.

- Never forget to throw a banana peel in her path.

- Never, ever, ever, EVER invite her over to your house.

35.

ARE YOU A SUPERMOM?

1. Since having children, my appearance has:

   A. Improved considerably. Being a mother has encouraged me to look better than ever for my husband and children. Almost every day, I'm stopped by someone who is truly amazed at the new me!

   B. Remained the same.

   C. Slipped substantially.

2. When I have free time, I:

   A. Put on a one-woman show of *Guys and Dolls* at the local nursing home as well as volunteer for duty at the downtown soup kitchen.

   B. Cut out recipes from magazines.

   C. Sleep.

3. When my children aren't napping, we typically:

   A. Get so involved in an ultra-creative, multi-media, three-dimensional craft project, we lose all track of time.

   B. Run errands.

   C. Pick the gum out of each other's hair.

4. For dinner, I usually:

   A. Fix a four-course, low-fat, nutritionally balanced gourmet meal plucked straight from the pages of *Eating Light*. (P.S. My kids always beg for seconds.)

   B. Boil pasta and pour bottled sauce over it.

   C. Reheat yesterday's take-out pizza in the microwave.

5. For Halloween, my child's costume was:

   A. A Teenage Mutant Ninja Turtle that I designed and sewed myself—months in advance.

   B. A ghost.

   C. Whatever was left on the drugstore shelf.

6.   The inside of my car looks like:

   A.   I could escort the King and Queen of England to a glorious ball. Since I don't allow my kids to eat in the car, I defy anyone to find a crumb.

   B.   A typical parent's car: a few crumbs, a few toys, a few greasy finger marks.

   C.   Some sort of foul swamp creature has moved in and reproduced.

SCORING:

For each A answer, give yourself 100 points. For each B, give yourself 50 points. For each C, give yourself one point. If your score is:

0-6   You are not a Supermom.

7-550   You are still not a Supermom.

600   TA-DA! YOU ARE A SUPERMOM!
          Happy? Well, big deal. Nobody else gives a s--t!

36.

ODE TO THE SUPERMOM

Oh Supermom, Supermom,
you make us feel so small;
Your house is much too clean,
and you're always on the ball.

You wash your sheets weekly,
with a happy-go-lucky smile;
You scrub your toilets brightly,
there's no mildew on your tile.

Oh Supermom, Supermom,
we want your perfect hair;
We want the fact that when you walk,
men still stop and stare.

Stretched-out leggings with no elastic,
are out of the question for you;
Shrunken sweaters sporting spittle,
will simply never do.

Oh Supermom, Supermom,
your control drives us batty;
Twinkies never tempt you,
and Fritos are too fatty.

So unlike the rest of us,
who eat their children's scraps;
You toss them down the drain, of course,
lest you sprout two laps.

Oh Supermom, Supermom,
we crave your mothering skills;
You handle tantrums with aplomb,
and embrace their trying wills.

You never spank, you never yell,
you never count to three;
Your children gladly share their toys,
and pick them up with glee.

Oh Supermom, Supermom,
we resent your self-reliance;
Where on earth did you learn,
to fix a broke appliance?

Yes! You hang your wallpaper,
of course you prune your shrubs;
Darn right! You seal your driveway,
and control those nasty grubs.

We hate to interrupt you,
but we've got a great big question:
How come you're so freaking happy,
when we've got indigestion?

37.

STAY-AT-HOME MOMS' EXCHANGE
(Great tips from moms who've been around the block)

"Leave your garage door up when you can. It shows there's life inside! And life inside means a potential friend."

Sandi Fisher, Marion, OH

"Never, ever, EVER wear a T-shirt that reads: 'Born to Shop.' Trust me, you'll never live it down."

Karen Horton, Buffalo, NY

"Next time someone yawns when they hear you're a full-time mom, peer deeply into their mouth and cry: 'Wow! You've got stage-three gum disease!'"

Ann Nelson, Reno, NV

"Never make friends with a mom whose house is a lot cleaner than yours. Why torture yourself with feelings of inadequacy?"

         Terri Ritter, NYC, NY

"Memorize a slew of bawdy jokes. Just because we're at-home moms doesn't mean we're holier-than-thou!"

         Suzy Case, Montclair, NJ

"Always check your feet before you leave the house. It's not uncommon for new tired moms to arrive at the grocery store wearing slippers."

         Erin Ryan, Bangor, ME

"Mum's the word if your baby takes four-hour naps. This information makes less-fortunate mom's blood boil!"

         Sue Best, Fairfield, CT

"Always leave one household chore to be completed when your husband is home. That way, he'll witness just how hard you work!"

         Mary Davis, Regina, MT

"Never brag about your superior baby's superior development. You'll lose friends faster than Linda Tripp."

         Gwenn Walters, Ukiah, CA

"Find something, anything, to laugh about each day. Nothing raises the spirits quite like a good giggle!"

         Ellen Mahoney, Boulder, CO

PART 7

BEAUTY TIPS,
AILMENTS,
MAKEOVERS,
AND MORE

LET'S
GET PHYSICAL

38.

CAN WE TALK?

When I traded in my pumps for Play-Doh, something happened to my appearance. It went, in the words of a small child, "Bye-Bye." Granted, my body had recently been put through a ringer of frightening physical changes. And true enough, the few strands of hair that remained on my head would never cooperate. And, yes, my desire to flaunt the latest fashions slowly but surely fizzled without the specter of Monday-morning meetings on my postnatal horizon.

But to care so little? So soon? Was it at all justified?

I am here now to say YES. I had more important things to think about, like diaper rash, cradle cap, and baths fraught with screams.

Not to mention, fevers, formula, and a phone that never rang.

Looking fabulous? At home? No, it wasn't high on my list of "Things To Do."   In fact, it never occurred to me that the two could go together, should go together, or ever would go together.

What's the point?

Well, now that I've been home a while, I'll tell you what the point is. When you feel better about the way you look, you can be a lot more assertive in public. And that's something to aspire to, especially when you're angling for fresh bagels in a jam-packed bakery or vying for the last Mr. Bubble tickets in a lobby full of raving mom-a-tics.

There's a great big hitch, however, when it comes to perking up your at-home appearance: No time. No time to diet. No time to exercise. No time to shower.

Believe me, I know all about "no-time" beauty regimes. For me, it was slapping on a pair of sunglasses and a baseball cap. But after a while, I wanted more. I wanted, for example, to lose those two hams strapped to my hiney.

So I turned to the resource nearest and dearest to my heart— MY HOME—and devised some sorta-clever-sorta-silly ways to lose weight (The Scrapsdale Diet), firm up (Mommercise), look presentable in under a minute (The One-Minute Makeover), and fashion an entire wardrobe out of sweats.

Who cares if the AMA, FDA, or PTA wouldn't endorse any of my plans—they worked for me. And I got to laugh along the way. What more could a mother ask for? (Well, actually . . . there's a lot more, but that's another book.)

39.

LOSE WEIGHT WITH THE SCRAPSDALE DIET

Trying to lose weight, as we all know, is no day at the beach. Trying to lose pregnancy weight—a unique form of weight that has been scientifically proven to possess a staying power greater than unwanted relatives—is definitely no day at the beach. But trying to lose pregnancy weight from a place of employment that boasts a toaster, an oven, and a stocked pantry? Well, heck, why not just throw us into a vat of chocolate and say, "Don't lick."

Consider the challenges:

- Not only must we shop for food, but we must then put away such irresistible items as heavenly half-melted ice cream.

- Not only must we prepare meals, but we, as conscientious mothers, must then sample them to ensure our concoctions are edible.

- Not only must we do the dishes, but we must then come face to face with perfectly acceptable uneaten pieces of fresh apple pie.

Who can resist? And get this, I haven't even mentioned the greatest obstacle of all: BEATERS LADEN WITH COOKIE DOUGH!

My downfall was ingesting the kiddo's scraps. So what I did was develop a diet plan that allowed me to scarf the scraps and not pack on the L-Bs. It's called, appropriately enough, The Scrapsdale Diet.

My plan is a cinch to follow. Unlike other diets, there's no counting fat grams here, no tricky combinations of foods, and no chewing each bite one hundred times. What's more—and probably most important—you won't get that stinky-winky bad breath associated with so many diets. All you do is finish the scraps the rugrats leave behind.

Is it for you? Answer the following questions and you'll know in a jiffy.

GOOD-CANDIDATE QUIZ FOR THE SCRAPSDALE DIET

1. Do you typically eat leftover crusts?

2. Have you ever slurped up the ice cream melting down Junior's cone?

3. Have you ever slurped up the ice cream melting down Junior's cone with the blind fury of an emaciated coyote wandering alone in the desert heat?

4. Do you ever polish off the half-eaten Twinkie found in your kid's lunch box, even though it has the imprint of a sneaker on it?

5. Do you find cold, soggy french fries incredibly tasty?

6. Do you find rock-hard french fries found under the back seat of your car even more appetizing?

7. Do you lick the peanut butter knife after making a sandwich and then redip it?

8. Have you ever wrestled the dog for a scrap of the kids' food, like, say, that last bite of a Snickers bar?

9. Do you lie awake at night thinking about that M&M you spotted under the couch?

10. Do you jokingly call yourself the "family goat" as you nibble on scraps before tossing them down the drain?

Moms, if you've answered "Yes" to even one of these questions, chances are my Scrapsdale Diet is the diet plan for you. Check below for a typical day's calories. And remember, scraps are your only meals.

Breakfast	Approx. Cal.
2 bread crusts rolled in a ball	30
1 fried egg yolk stuck to a napkin	80
6 Lucky Charms floating in 4 oz milk	60
4 Pop-Tart corners	10
BREAKFAST TOTAL	**180**

Snack

1 gnarled teething biscuit	15
Mutilated banana	40
Peanut butter scraped off a chin	20
SNACK TOTAL	**75**

Lunch

¼ tuna sandwich flattened by a fist	60
1 apple minus a bite	75
2 cheese doodles pulled from a nose	20
3 Oreo cookies minus the cream	60
4 ounces chocolate milk with pepper on top	50
LUNCH TOTAL	**265**

Snack

1 mangled marshmallow pulled from hair	15
1 nibbled-on graham cracker	15
SNACK TOTAL	**30**

Dinner

4 pizza crusts retrieved from floor	80
2 untouched bowls of pears	200
1 bowl of mashed lima beans	100
2 ounces milk with pepperoni boats	50
1 teaspoon of melted ice cream	5
1 M&M	5
DINNER TOTAL	**440**

Total calories for one day:	**990**

40.

FIGHT THE FLAB WITH MOMMERCISE

A s you can well imagine, firming up skin that has been stretched from here to kingdom come is no small task. Trust me, I know, having once been the not-so-proud owner of a deflated tummy that flopped around like a sneaker in the dryer.

I'm happy to report that my ab-flab is gone now and I can only thank my new stay-at-home life. Yes, it's true. Staying home to raise children causes women to burn a gargantuan amount of energy, so much so, that I cancelled my gym membership, tossed my exercise tapes out the window, and never watched those annoying aerobics shows again.

In fact, I don't even consciously think about exercise anymore. All I do now is Mommercise—and it's all you need to do, too.

Below are some typical at-home Mommercise activities and the calories expended per hour while performing them.

Activity: Coffee

Making coffee	100
Drinking coffee	125
Microwaving cold coffee	150
Discovering you're clean out of coffee	900

Activity: Leafing through catalogs

Perusing *Victoria's Secret* catalog	100
Perusing *Victoria's Secret* catalog while painstakingly searching for thigh cellulite	300
Perusing *Victoria's Secret* catalog while imagining hubby running off with sexy model	700
Yanking catalog from leering husband's clutches	900

Activity: Discipline

Calmly asking child to stop biting your calf	50
Gently placing child on "time-out" chair	100
Tackling child who has escaped from chair	300
Reseating squirming child	400
Threatening to burn toys if child moves	500
Bursting vein in forehead	1000

Activity: Playing

Pushing child on park swing	300
Pushing child who demands that you sing "Three Blind Mice" while swinging	600

Prying resistant child from park swing while dodging kicks	900
Pretending not to notice that a crowd of mothers has gathered to criticize you.	50

Activity: Daily Chores

Using toes to sort laundry	100
Untying a pesky sneaker knot	200
Scraping Gak off window	300
Tackling a tenacious Tang stain	400
Chiseling hardened goo off high chair	800
Extracting burrs from screaming child's hair	1000
Dislodging child's head from stair banister	2000
Pacing madly, wondering what to fix for dinner	3000
Boiling pasta (again)	50

Activity: Bathrooms

Noticing bathroom is foul and needs cleaning	100
Rationalizing that it can wait another week	200
Realizing that you made that same rationalization last week and the week before	300
Feeling like you're a disgusting individual with no sense of hygiene whatsoever	400
Stepping on urine-soaked Ninja undies as you race from the bathroom holding your nose	500
Resolving to try again tomorrow	0

41.

ONE MINUTE STAY-AT-HOME MAKEOVER

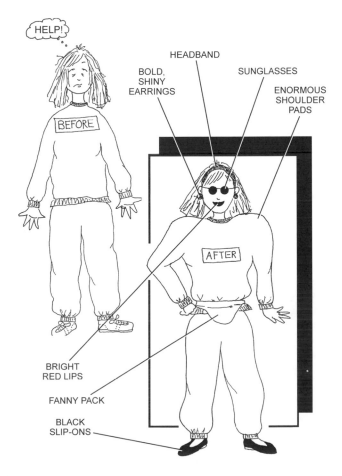

1. **Headband:**
   Creates hairstyle with no effort. Great for dirty hair.

2. **Sunglasses:**
   Take you from harried to hip in seconds. Terrific for hiding dark circles.

3. **Bold, Shiny Earrings:**
   Perk up entire face.

4. **Bright Red Lips:**
   No lipstick? Slurp Juicy Juice for lasting color.

5. **Enormous Shoulder Pads:**
   Add instant power. The bigger the better!
   (OK to use diapers in a pinch.)

6. **Fanny Pack:**
   Gives waist definition.

7. **Black Slip-Ons:**
   Final stab at style.

42.

HAIR TIPS FROM A BAD-HAIR-YEAR VETERAN

The biggest hair tip I can give to you, new mothers, is a simple one: *Do not dramatically alter your hairstyle during your first year at home.* Do what you want your second year, after your wildly fluctuating first-year hormones have settled. But your first year? Leave those locks alone. Invest in headbands, bows, and cool baseball caps. Just don't chop it all off.

Oh, you'll be tempted. You'll look in the mirror one morning and think: Maybe this mop would look better a little shorter. Maybe it would be easier to take care of. Maybe my baby won't have so much to grab in that bionic fist. Maybe, just maybe, I'd get a little more respect with shorter hair.

But I say from experience, fight the temptation. Otherwise, you may be in for a whole lot of tears: from regret, from a lousy cut, from giving your heart and soul over to motherhood in a way you vowed you never would, from whatever!

If you're still tempted, I urge you to review some of the good reasons I've provided below for NOT changing your current hairstyle.

SIX GOOD REASONS TO MAINTAIN STATUS-[hair]-QUO

1. Everybody is expecting YOU, a new mother brimming with maternal instincts and overflowing with milk, to adopt a more practical, sedate style. Fool them.

2. Cutting your hair does not, I repeat, does not make you and your baby look more alike. If anything, it may make you look more like its daddy.

3. Lopping your locks often precipitates getting a perm, which then precipitates spending even more time to right the perm, which then precipitates a full-blown migraine. Why bother?

4. Slightly longer hair is actually easier to maintain, and when pulled back in a tight ponytail, it has the added benefit of providing a faux facelift.

5. Shorter hair and maturity do not go hand in hand. If you're irreverent now, trust me, you'll be even worse with no hair to hide behind.

6. Getting your hair cut takes time. Have you forgotten? You don't have any time!

MY BAD-HAIR-YEAR REVISITED

Month 1:

> *"I hate my body, I hate my clothes, I hate it when people say my baby looks exactly like my husband, and I really hate my hair."*

Month 2:

> *"Yeah, I cut bangs for a little interest around my face. My God, they're so annoying."*

Month 3:

> *"Oh, that mark? Well, I scorched the livin' life out of my forehead with my stupid curling iron. These bangs are the pits."*

Month 4:

> *"Me? D'ya really think I look like the Campbell's Soup girl? Geez, all I did was shorten it a little!"*

Month 5:

> *"No, for crying out loud, I'm Mrs. Palumbo, the mother!"*

Month 6:

> *"Boy do I regret this short style. Grows faster than a freaking weed on Miracle-Gro. What choice do I have but to buzz it myself?"*

Month 7:

> *"Yeah, I figured a perm would make things a little easier. And, no, I do not appreciate being called a 'poodle head'."*

Month 8:

> *"Remember that perm? Well, it charred my hair to smithereens. Boo hoo hoo, I've never cried so hard in my life."*

Month 9:

"Really? You honestly think babypoo and I look alike? Well, gee, it only took going bald from a perm to reach this satisfying point."

Month 10:

"Honey, can I ask you a little favor? NEVER say I look like my mother again."

Month 11:

"Don't tell a soul. I'm wearing 20 hair extensions. Cool, huh?"

Month 12:

"No, I won't be cutting my hair for quite a long time. One year of torture was enough for me, thank you."

43.

OUT WITH STOCKINGS . . . IN WITH THE SWEATS

Not wearing stockings during the day was an unexpected bonus when I became a Stay-at-Home Mom. Did I say unexpected bonus? Heck, what I meant to say was, an unexpected bonanza of joyful, unencumbered bliss that rivaled swimming naked in a sea of loose change.

No, I never liked pantyhose, especially in the sweltering summer when they clung to me like tar on asphalt. And you know, they often betrayed me, especially around sharp-edged filing cabinets before important meetings. So you can imagine how thrilled I was when sweats, big comfy sweats, became my wardrobe staple.

Oh, I know. Many people think sweats are ugly, an open admission you've thrown in the towel, a red carpet to Rotundville.

Not so! Sweats are every mom's dream separate. They're comfortable around our ever-fluctuating waists. They're absorbent around our little one's ever-fluctuating diaper. They're wrinkle-free, which is nice when we pull them up off the floor to wear again. And they hide stains, which is a miracle in and of itself.

What's more, sweats can be stylish, flattering, and even—yes, even—sexy. All you need is a sharp pair of scissors, a leaf shredder, and an ability to throw caution to the wind.

Take a look at some of the snappy sweats I've designed and I bet you'll be sharpening those scissors in seconds flat.

"CHER" BELL-BOTTOM SWEATS

This style is ideal for all you long, lean mommy machines. Top with a ruffly white shirt for a look that will turn heads at the local library. To make: Insert a hemorrhoidal donut ring into each pant leg and inflate.

VICTORIA'S SECRET SWEATS

Shorter than your shortest shorts, this is the sweat to wear when you crave a breeze but feel too lazy to zip up those boring culottes. Likewise, there's no better sweat to don when wading through flooded basements. To make: Cut off both legs at crotch with pinking shears.

TUXEDO SWEATS

Cropped in the front and flowing in the back, these sweats are the best choice for those kinda-cool-kinda-warm-kinda-confusing kinds of days. The backflaps are excellent for dragging limp kids suffering from the "noodle syndrome" through stores. To make: Lop off the front until your knees show.

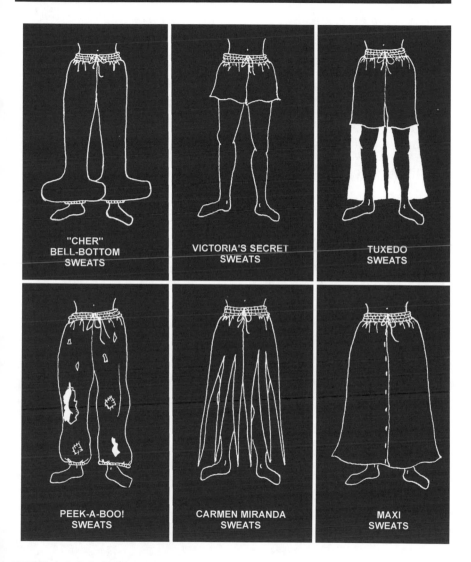

"CHER"
BELL-BOTTOM
SWEATS

VICTORIA'S SECRET
SWEATS

TUXEDO
SWEATS

PEEK-A-BOO!
SWEATS

CARMEN MIRANDA
SWEATS

MAXI
SWEATS

PEEK-A-BOO SWEATS

Own any ratty sweats? Don't throw them away! The
"grunge" look is today's hottest fashion statement and it
doesn't seem to be going anywhere. Suede clogs and a
crocheted top complete this fab look. If you need to
make: Fling spoonfuls of Clorox on each leg.

CARMEN MIRANDA SWEATS

These frisky, frothy sweats are your answer to that agonizing question: "What should I wear tonight?" Accessorize with a couple of bananas on your head and you'll be the hit of the party. To make: Insert sweats into a leaf shredder; stop before crotch.

MAXI SWEATS

This groovy style is a natch for outdoor rock concerts and for sneaking kids into matinees. Make them the same way you made that boss jean skirt in high school. Top with a gauze shirt, crank up some Judy Collins, and you'll be in flashback heaven.

MADONNA SWEATS (NOT SHOWN)

Voila! All you need is the drawstring!

44.

COMMON AILMENTS OF STAY-AT-HOME MOMS

Not so long ago, you were probably riding high on the horse of health with a little tennis here, a little aerobics there. Colds, coughs, aches, and pains weren't even a part of your vocabulary, were they? I ask you now: Does a day go by when you're not felled by yet another new pain, or at least consumed by the horror of catching yet another cold?

If it makes you feel any better, most new mothers experience enough ailments to warrant a vaccine their first few years at home. I certainly did. In fact, the diagram on the next page is really me, on one of my better days. The only thing you don't see is the chronic complaining that accompanied each ailment—a habit that, though annoying, always brought me reams of relief.

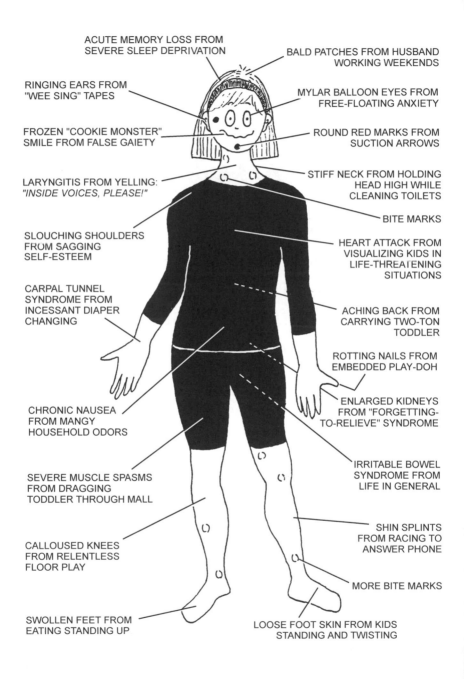

PART 8

BOREDOM, BURNOUT, MYTHS, AND MORE

THE
DOWNSIDE

45.

MORE BORING THAN . . .

I have a confession to make. There are times—big chunks of time actually—when staying home can be utterly and incredibly B-O-R-I-N-G. More boring than listening to someone drone on and on about a silly dream that has nothing to do with you. More boring than standing around at a stuffy cocktail party listening to accountants say things like, "Now, to make a long story short . . ." More boring, in fact, than almost anything we ever did before we had kids.

Please don't misunderstand. I love my children and adore watching them grow, play, and beat each other silly over something stupid like who gets the last rock-hard marshmallow.

I'm not talking about that. Heck, no. I'm referring to the day-in-day-out-what's-up?-not-much boredom. The boredom that each and every Stay-at-Home Mom eventually feels all the way down to her aching roots. The boredom, ahem, you'll soon discover no one talks about. THAT boredom.

Why doesn't anybody talk about it? Well, who knows really. Maybe it's because we feel a little guilty associating tedium with child rearing. Maybe it's because we never anticipated just how monotonous stay-at-home life could be. Maybe it's because we don't want to reveal how boring it is for fear people will then assume we're boring. Or maybe, just maybe, it's because we think we're the only one out there with a permanent yawn creeping across our face.

Moms, think again. I can tell you from experience, there is simply no mother who screams "hallelujah" at the prospect of changing another wicked diaper. There is simply NO mother who:

- fandangos her way out to mow the lawn.

- is mentally inspired when it comes to cleaning toilets, sorting socks, or dusting furniture.

- giggles with glee as she confronts yet another bed to make.

- looks forward to playing CandyLand again and again and AGAIN.

So there. I admitted it. *Staying at home can be boring.* And, yes, it's true, there are times when I feel boring for staying in my boring house so much of the boring time performing so many boring tasks. But I am not dull. And neither are you. It's the dreary chores that are duller than dishwater.

46.

ODE TO BOREDOM

The daily chores we do . . . fill our limbs with lead.
The daily chores we do . . . empty out our head.

The daily chores we do . . . turn us into slaves.
The daily chores we do . . . add light-years to our days.

The daily chores we do . . . swell our aching feet.
The daily chores we do . . . are anything but sweet.

The daily chores we do . . . are necessities of life.
The daily chores we do . . . make us want a Rent-a-Wife!

47.

COPING WITH STAY-AT-HOME BURNOUT

Sometime around your second or third year of staying home (maybe sooner for some), don't be surprised if you experience a "sinking" feeling and then, little by little, completely burn out. It happens to the best of us, and though usually short-lived, it's virtually unavoidable.

How will you know when you're at your wit's end? Believe me, you'll know.

Where once it was perfectly acceptable for the kids to empty the pots-and-pans cupboard during the height of meal preparation, now an innocent request for water elicits a sharp, "NOT NOW!"

Where once you placated their need to crawl all over you while you were on the phone, now you keep them at bay with one hand, one foot, or possibly both feet planted on their insistent little foreheads.

Where once you allowed them to dillydally their way into the car, now, at the first sign of resistance, you firmly wedge your foot between their dawdling legs and give them the old heave-ho straight through the window.

Where once you were the first in line to see Chuckles the Clown, now you can barely sit through a performance without shouting, "Get a real job, Chuckhead!"

But that's not all. Seemingly benign events will send you into uncontrollable, unbelievable, unwarranted fits of rage: a shopping cart with a bum wheel, a Brownie badge to stitch on, a cupcake to frost, or a happy mother in the park.

As a word of warning, when it hits, this end-of-your-rope feeling will be overwhelming. You will feel like every single, eentsy-weentsy drop of patience has been squeezed from your exhausted body. You will feel like strangling the next person who starts a sentence with, "Could you . . ." And you will especially feel like no one appreciates you, no one has ever appreciated you, and no one will ever, ever, EVER appreciate you enough.

Even worse, you may find yourself unusually drawn to obituaries during this bleak time, seeking out the particularly long ones about remarkable women who had more hobbies than Martha Stewart, more degrees than Hillary Clinton, and more children than Rose Kennedy. Forget that you don't know the stiffs; their achievements alone flabbergast you, sending you into a downward spiral of self-doubt.

And then it will finally happen. You'll wake up one morning without an ounce left to give, without a smile on your face, without a nail to call your own. "Now what?" you'll wail from the bed you refuse to leave. "N-O-O-O-W WHA-A-A-A-A-T?"

THE CURE FOR STAY-AT-HOME BURNOUT

Listen carefully. Here's exactly what you'll need to do to get through this wretched time:

1. Pack your bags—ASAP—and go away for the weekend with your best female friend. Although you've probably grown quite fond of your beloved sweats, leave them home if you can and pack something with a little more pizzazz.

2. Have fun: laugh, share secrets, tell jokes, shop, eat at great restaurants, and by all means be sure to quench your thirst in a meaningful way.

3. Upon return (I'm assuming you will), make a list of everything you used to do that made you happy. Note: Your paper may be blank for some time since "getting the children to sleep through the night" has been your chief source of happiness for years—but stick with it.

4. Sit down with your husband and discuss how you plan to accomplish some of these happiness ventures. Being the great guy that he always says he is, he'll probably agree to support you and watch the kids more often.

    Note: With obstinate, unsupportive husbands, try this technique:

    > Describe in giddy detail the dream you had about giving birth to a van-load of kids. Then wistfully say, "Oh, how I wish it would come

true." Most likely, he'll be hauling those kids off to the museum before you can say, "Don't forget the juice."

5.   Just do it.

48.

10 MOST COMMON MYTHS ABOUT STAY-AT-HOME MOMS

1. **Myth:**   We watch TV all day long.

   Fact: Gimme a break. We've got better things to do than plant ourselves in front of the tube all day. For example, we've got KIDS TO RAISE.

2. **Myth:**   We like to clean.

   Fact: Hmmm, let's see now. Would we rather clean the house, or swim naked with starving piranhas? Hands down winner: Swim with the fish.

3.　**Myth:**　We love being the flower- and UPS-drop box for the neighborhood.

　　Fact:　No, we do not love being the "catch-all" for everybody's stuff. Vicariously experiencing our neighbors' flowers and direct-mail goodies is not our idea of a good time . . . at all.

4.　**Myth:**　We sincerely dig Tupperware parties.

　　Fact:　Negative. We're no different than the rest of the human race—we resent going, too. If we do attend, it's for one and only one reason: so our husbands will put the crank-meisters to bed.

5.　**Myth:**　We're at home because we can't cut it in the "real" world.

　　Fact:　You know what? Most of us have already swathed that path. Our job now is much more important, although I must say the pay sucks.

6.　**Myth:**　We transform into *Goody-Two-Shoes* over time.

　　Fact:　Honestly! The vile, despicable thoughts that cross our minds would curl a priest's teeth!

7.　**Myth:**　We talk on the phone all day.

　　Fact:　No; not all day. But, yes, we do reach out when our patience has evaporated, our metabolism is near death, our hair has gone flat, and an annoying neighbor with a contribution envelope is pounding on the door.

8. **Myth:** We are all fundamentally lazy.

   Fact: Meeting the needs of growing, restless, thirsty children requires more energy than it takes to blast an Apollo into outer space, more stamina than it takes to scale Mt. Kilimanjaro in 200 mph winds, and more courage than it takes to marry Michael Jackson. Have I made myself perfectly clear?

9. **Myth:** We all love Barney.

   Fact: Some adore that great big purple blob. Some abhor that great big purple blob. But it's "The Professor" from *Gilligan's Island* that most moms love, not Barney.

10. **Myth:** We putz around in dusters, mules, and sponge rollers.

    Fact: Sorr-e-e-e. As far as I know, only those rural mothers on TV who live in the remote hills of Kookamonga wear that awful garb.

49.

FIVE WAYS TO HOLD YOUR HEAD HIGH WHILE CLEANING A TOILET

1. Clean it from a ladder.

2. Pretend you're cleaning King Tut's tomb.

3. Clean it while engaged in other mind-bending tasks.

4. Clean it with a dictionary on your head.

5. Simply refuse to clean it!

50.

HOW TO SHAKE THE JUNE CLEAVER RAP

At some point in your illustrious stay-at-home career, someone will probably refer to you as "June Cleaver." I am here to tell you now, with the Beave as my witness, that it isn't a compliment. No, it's a stay-at-home slam of the worst kind, a snide little reference meant to undermine your Herculean efforts to keep the fires burning.

You see, June is no longered revered. She's a metaphor now. And you want to know what that metaphor stands for? Why, it stands for a complacent homemaker full of half-baked ideas; it stands for a Pollyanna who'll babysit all the world's children at the drop of a hat; it stands for someone who's so out of it, they clean in a dress.

Take it from me, you don't want to be called June Cleaver. Ever. So it's important that you walk tall, hold your head high, and ditch any of those meek little habits that seem to attach themselves to "moms on the verge"—if you know what I mean.

Check the following chart for the kinds of habits that keep moms in June's ancient clutches. Next to each old habit, you'll find a new habit that you should considering honing, that is, if you'd like to dramatically upgrade your stay-at-home status.

OLD AT-HOME HABITS	NEW AT-HOME HABITS
EACH TIME YOU SLIP INTO ONE OF THESE, PUT YOUR WET HAND IN THE FREEZER AND HOLD FOR 10 MINUTES.	*EACH TIME YOU TRY ONE OF THESE, REWARD YOURSELF WITH A GIGANTIC TIME-OUT FOR MOM.*
Looking down shamefully when asked what you do.	Establishing black-as-thunder eye contact when someone inquires about your job status.
Clearing dishes at the neighborhood block party with a dutiful smile.	Challenging anyone within spitting distance to an arm wrestle.
Speaking so softly that no one can hear what you say.	Spraying saliva as you passionately unload whatever needs unloading.
Humming "Que Sera, Sera" as you serenely vacuum.	Wailing "Another One Bites the Dust" as you vacuum in roller blades at break-neck speed.

OLD AT-HOME HABITS	NEW AT-HOME HABITS
Buying truckloads of Tupperware out of spineless obligation.	Refusing to buy the stuff on the grounds that you've already melted over 1,000 tops in your dishwasher.
Thinking that, next to Windex, Pine-Sol is life's most intoxicating scent.	Concluding that anyone's home that smells antiseptic suffers from a grave anal-retentive disorder.
Blinking back jubilant tears when asked to volunteer yet another 100 hours of community service.	Shrieking, "Sure, I'll volunteer, no problem. But this time I want cash for my efforts, cuz I'm worth it!"
Sending the next-door-neighbor kid home with a plate full of cookies, freshly whitened sneakers, and your last coupon for free pizza.	Demanding that the ingrate come loaded with popcorn and a video next time he shows his mug.
Slipping blissfully into a velour lounger before retrieving the morning newspaper.	Struttin' out to get the paper in a Grateful Dead T-shirt, fuschia undies, and cowboy boots.
Driving below the speed limit.	Gunning your engine at stoplights—with your radio cranked full blast!

51.

STAY-AT-HOME SYNDROMES TO AVOID

As mothers, we all have days when we are simply not ourselves. We may complain a little too loud, cry a little too hard, clean a little too much, and smile a little too falsely. But as with a smelly diaper pail, these oddball behaviors can be easily dismissed with the wave of a hand.

There are some mothers, however, who fall prey to certain behaviors and then incorporate them into their daily lives. Who knows why this happens, but once it does, WATCH OUT! A syndrome is about to set in.

Take a look at some of the most common stay-at-home syndromes described below. You might see someone you know, or better, someone you can help, or even better than that, someone you can talk about behind their back. Just kidding. Of course we don't talk about mothers behind their backs. Well, at least not the stay-at-home kind.

THE ANN LANDERS SYNDROME

Moms who suffer from this syndrome are a geyser of useful information, tips, hints, suggestions, and advice. The only problem is, they don't know how to mind their own business and quit their spoutin'. It's not uncommon for them to walk into someone's home and say something like: "My baby used to be that fat, but then I switched to 2%," or "Didn't you know you're not supposed to microwave formula? Geez! Wake up and smell the coffee!" And heaven help the friends who actually ask for advice. The amount of information released by sufferers of this syndrome could blow an eyebrow to Iceland.

How to help the afflicted: Quietly leave the room in the middle of her informational tirade and return with a stick of gum.

THE RED-HOT MAMA SYNDROME

It's not too tough to spot a mom suffering from this "I'm-still-sexy-aren't-I?" syndrome. They're the mamas wearing high heels with cutoffs to Toys 'R' Us . . . the sizzlers sporting minis at the local McDonald's . . . the show-offs strutting around the community pool in a thong bikini. Convinced that all hormones escaped when Boomer was born, they are consumed with appearing sexy to the world. Too bad they make the rest of us cringe.

How to help the afflicted: Hand her a terry cover-up and a big glass of wholesome milk.

THE MARY TYLER MOORE SYNDROME

Moms in the thralls of this high-spirited syndrome are so happy they make birds sing in a blizzard. Up all night with a sick child? Won't crack the smile on their cheery faces. Postman run over their award-winning roses? Accidents happen. Husband late for dinner three nights in a row? "He's the breadwinner," they say in giddy defense. Yesiree, everyone can always count on these moms for a round-the-clock smile. But because being home and being chronically happy do not go hand in hand, we're all a little confused, if not frightened, by the M-T-M Mom's behavior.

How to help the afflicted: Urge her to complain, complain, and then COMPLAIN some more.

THE I'M SORRY SYNDROME

Sufferers of this insipid syndrome are darn near sorry about everything. They're sorry the dry cleaners shrunk their favorite dress. "Must be the fabric, sorry." They're sorry the hairdresser dyed their hair the color of a pumpkin. "Must have weird hair, sorry." Why, they're even sorry their husband sideswiped the garage. "The garage is obviously too narrow. Sorrr-eeeee." It's the most frustrating syndrome because the words "I'm sorry" come so naturally to those in a vulnerable, frazzled state.

How to help the afflicted: Advise her to memorize these words, "Staying home means never having to say you're sorry."

THE DAUGHTERS OF THE AMERICAN REVOLUTION SYNDROME

Stranger things have happened to women who become mothers, but none so strange as the D.A.R. syndrome. Neatly wrapping all past vices and pleasures into a tidy, never-to-be-opened package, sufferers perch themselves on every volunteer board this side of Mars and begin their life anew. They grocery shop in pleated skirts and patent leathers, wrinkle their nose at the least offensive joke, shun alcohol with the conviction of a saint, and walk with their buttocks tightly clenched.

How to help the afflicted: Suggest she devote at least two hours a day to "hugging," lest mommy-rigor-mortis sets in.

THE LITTLE SUZY HOMEMAKER SYNDROME

"A woman's work is never done." So goes the motto of moms who transform into Little Suzy Homemaker over time. At the crack of the morning whip, they tackle household chores with the tenacity of a pit bull, the speed of a humming bird, the happiness of a lark. Holy Toledo! They bake bread, sew wardrobes, install carpets, pour sidewalks, build sunrooms, clean gutters, plant pine trees, and, of course, never sit down.

How to help the afflicted: Give her some roses and remind her they're for smelling—not pruning.

THE MOM-GONE-BAD SYNDROME

Like a fine wine that turns to vinegar when left uncorked, moms embroiled in this wicked syndrome make Roseanne look like Snow White. Unhappy with being home full time, they pick fights with neighbors, toss diapers from windows, and stroll with a snarl that makes dogs run for cover. No, you won't want to cross this mom's path. She might douse you with a Super Soaker or take a pogo stick to your direct-from-Holland tulips. Her favorite hobby? Doing "360s" in the church parking lot, what else?

How to help the afflicted: Gently suggest to her that having another child might not be such a good idea after all.

PART 9

THE TRUTH ABOUT PLAYGROUPS, PARKS, VACATIONS . . . AND THE LIKE

THE INSIDE SCOOP

52.

PLAYGROUPS:
TO JOIN OR NOT TO JOIN

When I was growing up, the concept of "organized play" didn't even exist. Mothers were home; kids ran wild; mothers would tear around the neighborhood, screaming, "Has anyone seen Leo?" and life went on. These days, however, "play" comes in a new, highly organized format: The playgroup. By now, you've probably heard of them, or may even be a participant in one. But for those of you who have no idea what they are, let me enlighten you:

playgroup *n* **1:** a bunch of screaming toddlers
and their desperate mothers who descend upon
your house, once a month, expecting food, fun,

and forgiveness (for the huge mess they make).
2: an activity that forces mothers to clean their
bathrooms on a regular basis.

The first playgroup I participated in was . . . oh, I don't know, not a good fit. Although I initially welcomed the regular socialization, I must confess, I gradually grew to loathe Le Group. Nobody ever talked about anything interesting. Here I was raring to share juicy tidbits about life, love, and the pursuit of postnatal bliss, and all we ever jawed about was home stuff: diapers, diarrhea, and drape treatments. Ugh. I knew it was time to drop out when I, in a burst of frustration, expressed my desire to engage in a threesome with Big Bird and Mr. Rogers . . . and, well, you can guess the rest.

My second shot at playgroups proved much more satisfying. We clicked, and as a result, felt comfortable sharing all sorts of scintillating information. What's more—after six months of investigative probing—I finally got my hands on that top-secret formula for whitening sneakers. Okay, here it is: ¼ cup Clorox, ¼ cup granulated dishwashing soap, ¼ cup Tide, and 4 cups water. Just mix and soak.

Should you join a playgroup? It's probably a good idea, especially if you're on the brink of entering that pathological stage of loneliness—the stage where you begin having in-depth arguments with inanimate objects. "Yo! Chair! Get outta my way! If I've told you once, I've told you a thousand times: MOVE."

To help you with your decision, I've provided some playgroup pros and cons. Take a look before you make the leap.

PROS:	CONS:
Encourages you to clean your house.	Forces you to clean when it's the last thing you want to do in the whole wide world.
Encourages you to socialize on a regular basis.	Forces you to spend oh-so-precious time with a few women you wouldn't befriend for all the Pampers in Panama.
Encourages you to bake goodies.	Forces you to feed a messy, ravenous group.
Encourages moms to express concerns about parenting, staying home, etc.	Forces you to listen to one bore who dominates with chronic gripes about her hemorrhoids.
Encourages children to share toys.	Forces kids to maniacally repress their natural tendencies of not wanting to share a thing.
Encourages you to dress nicely at least once a week.	Forces you to wear pants that are terribly tight around the waist: It's all you have that's acceptable!
Encourages you to observe how other women decorate.	Forces you to realize you have the decorating pizazz of a putz . . . or else, they do.
Encourages discussion about the effects of children on marriage.	Forces you to engage in a topic you find hopelessly depressing.

53.

PLAYGROUP ETIQUETTE

WHAT NOT TO SAY TO THE HOSTESS OF YOUR PLAYGROUP

"What smells?"

    OR

"Whoa! Talk about excess! I can't believe all the toys your kid has!"

    OR

"Decorating is just SO hard—have you ever considered enlisting the help of a professional?"

    OR

"Eeewww. What's this gooey stuff under the coffee table?"

OR

"Are you honestly going to make me reimburse you for the Hummel my son just broke?"

OR

"Would you mind if the kids jumped on your water bed?"

OR

"Whaddaya have to do to get a cup of coffee in this joint?"

OR

"Instant coffee? Ha, ha, ha. It's a joke, right?"

OR

"Now that's what I call interesting wallpaper. Came with the house, right? No? You actually picked it out yourself? Oh."

54.

GOING TO THE PARK

Parks are a curious phenomenon for the Stay-at-Home Mom. You would think there could be no better place in the world for meeting other moms. But it's not always the case.

Lots of moms are so wrapped up in their children they can't spare a breath to chat; or they purposely bring along monster weaving projects that totally monopolize their time. Sadly, I was one of those gotta-look-busy moms, lugging *War and Peace* everywhere I went. Well, guess what? No one bothered me, thinking I was more interested in reading than nurturing a stay-at-home friend.

Things changed for me, however, the day I got nailed in the nose with a Nerf ball, Unbelievably, that little, yellow, annoying ball forced me to get off my park bench and connect with the mother of the derelict who threw it. One thing led to another—and we've been friends ever since.

You might be wondering: Must a whack on the nose precede every friendship in the park setting? Of course not! That was just my sorry situation because I didn't know the . . . rules.

If you're striking out in the sandbox, take a look at the park rules my good friends Pat and Patty compiled for new, at-home moms.

PAT AND PATTY'S PARK RULES
FOR MAKING FAST FRIENDS

1. **No loud, happy singing:** Your false gaiety is a turnoff.

2. **No flirting with the maintenance men:** It's inappropriate and will make moms wonder where your allegiances lie.

3. **No 8' x 8' needlepoint project:** Your busy-as-a-beaver facade makes you unapproachable.

4. **No elaborate snacks:** You'll arouse jealousy among all the other moms who brought stale saltines and water.

5. **No halters:** No explanation needed.

6. **No climbing on the equipment:** Leave the fun to the kids, you big noodlehead. Besides, other moms will resent your high energy level.

7. **No suntanning:** You'll be branded an "airhead" and left alone.

8. **No laptop computers:** You'll be branded an "egghead" and left alone.

9. **No boomboxes:** They're too un-motherly for the innocent park setting. You'll scare mothers away—far, far away.

10. **No alcohol:** You'll either (1) raise suspicions about your fitness as a mother; or (?) cause someone to get trampled in the stampede of mothers rushing to tip a cold one.

55.

VACATIONS: THE GOOD, THE BAD, AND THE UGLY

Vacations will never be what they used to be, now that you have kids. Long gone are the good old days of dashing off to a charming country inn on the spur of the moment. Nope, these days, it's months of planning, weeks of packing, and days of traveling to a questionable-at-best vacation spot.

And to do what? Why, to clone the life you lead—right down to the last dirty diaper—only in someone else's inconvenient, clapboard cottage.

You can still remember that first disastrous vacation, can't you? The one where your hopes were naively high, the one where you incredulously expected a little R&R. How were you to know then that going on a family vacation really means quadrupling the workload for mom?

Or how about that horrendous vacation you took with that other couple and their kids? Can you bear to even dredge up the painful memories? (What? You say you destroyed all the film?) Not so surprisingly, you haven't spoken since, what with the way you both accused the other of raising demonic brats. And to think, you'd been best friends since grammar school.

And let's not forget that wretched camping trip where, thanks to the monsoon downpour, you spent ten days trapped in a tent eating nothing but beef jerky. Could your son's diapers have been more vile? Could you have come closer to strangling your husband with a bungee cord?

They say that "breaking up" is hard to do. Ha! Try going on a vacation with two kids under three, three kids under five, or four kids under six. Now that's hard to do! It's so hard, in fact, it requires a recovery period afterward.

So here are some tips for dealing with a vacation that's gone awry.

ADVICE FOR THE TRAVEL-WEARY

1. Acknowledge that vacations are work, not play, and unload the stabbing pain of disappointment. Weep, complain, nail someone with a sopping sponge. Let it out.

2. Keep in mind that the first vacation will be the hardest. Over time and with an unlimited supply of mood-altering beverages, they will become easier to withstand.

3. If you're in the midst of a particularly hard vacation, be sure to tell your family to respect your need to grieve—all alone—on the beach—for eight solid hours—with a "beerball" nearby.

4. If you're not ready to vacation again, don't. Well-meaning friends and family may try to arrange a tantalizing trip to the Tiddlywink Hall of Fame as soon as possible. But agree to vacation only when you're ready. (Exception: A one-way ticket to Tahiti.)

5. Recognize that there will be setbacks. Finding a dead conch in your son's suitcase will undoubtedly unleash a flood of painful vacation memories.

6. Try not to fantasize about other family's vacations. Not everyone can afford dude ranches, Club Med, and ski trips to Aspen . . . and even if they can, they're probably dysfunctional.

7. Consider bringing along a relative on your next vacation. Agree to pay their way, mention the word "bonding," and then saddle them with the kids for the entire time.

8. Keep busy. Tackle load after load of vacation laundry the second you return to avoid falling into a depressed state.

9. Remember: Living without ever having vacationed is a far greater tragedy. As hard as it may be for you to believe, you will one day vacation again. And if you're lucky, maybe then you'll contract Lyme disease and be left all alone.

56.

THE STAY-AT-HOME LUNCHEON

Sooner or later it will happen. You will be asked to attend the quintessential stay-at-home event, the event destined to transform you—once and for all—into your mother: The Ladies Luncheon.

The first thing you need to think about is whether or not you care to pursue this pastime. The way I see it, you have one of three choices when the invitation arrives:

1. **Ignore it.**
    If you choose to do this, know that you'll never be asked again and that you'll definitely be talked about behind

your back: "The unsociable snob—who does she think she is anyway?"

2. **Respond with a lengthy excuse about why you can't make it.**
    In this case, you may be asked one more time and you'll probably be talked about behind your back: "I don't know about this one; she could go either way. Anybody notice what kind of car she drives?"

3. **Accept the invitation.**
    Whether you want to go or not, "accepting" is usually your best option. But do understand that you'll be cooking sometime soon and that you'll possibly be talked about behind your back: "God, I hope she opens up a little. She's such a quiet thing."

I opted to go, despite my reservations that I would walk in with an attitude and walk out with an apron. But guess what? I had a hoot! Moms let loose. Kids were ignored. And we all felt like queens, eating such good food smack in the middle of the day.

Since then, I've attended several Ladies Luncheons and have given a few of my own. Although I prefer to be the "attendee," it's not so bad hosting one. You just need to know the skinny.

TIPS FOR THROWING A FABULOUS LUNCHEON:

- Don't ask if anyone wants a drink; assume they do. Instead, ask: "Red? White? Mad Dog 20/20?"

- Don't serve loud, crunchy foods. The topics moms are dying to discuss warrant whispering—lest you want those little ears in the next room to perk up. So serve soft foods like quiche or shrimp salad to promote optimum hearing and to encourage the kind of storytelling fit for *The Enquirer*.

- Hold back on the number of courses. Too many of them are intimidating, not to mention physically painful. Moms aren't accustomed to eating six-course meals in the middle of the day. Another very good reason for not stuffing your guests is that too much food will cancel the inebriating affects of the alcohol. Need I say more?

- Never forget the goal of your luncheon, which is to get moms to reveal their deepest, darkest secrets—along with anything spicy about their current lives. Thus, as the hostess, you must always steer the conversation clear of kiddie talk. Here's one way to get back on track:

  > Mom: "My son still doesn't sleep through the night . . . and he's six!"

  > Hostess: "You say you can't sleep because you're having too much sex?"

  > Mom: "What? I was talking about my son, not me."

  > Hostess: "You say your husband prefers to do it at three?"

  > Mom: "Three? What are you talking about?"

  > Hostess: "What time your husband likes to have sex."

  > Mom: "Oh, that. Let's see, he likes to . . ."

  > (and so on).

- Don't overdecorate, overdress, or go overboard preparing elaborate, gourmet meals. You will introduce a competitive edge to your luncheons; and, unless you're fond of stiff dining experiences, this is probably something you do not want to do.

- Don't fret if you can't find the time to prepare everything. Do what you can, buy what you can't, place whatever you bought in your pans, and then take credit for everything. If someone asks for a recipe, simply tell them you'll find it later, and then forget about it.

57.

OFF TO THE LIBRARY

You see a disheveled woman emerge from a building with wind-whipped hair, tousled clothing, and one shoe missing. She's also clutching a book under one arm and what appears to be a howling human bundle under the other. This makes you think:

   a.   She needs a new hairdresser

   b.   She's trying out for a part in *Terminator III*

   c.   She's spent yet another harrowing hour at the library

If you answered "c," you answered correctly. Almost no mom emerges unscathed from a trip to the House of Shhhh. In fact, most moms view going to the library with small, hush-resistant children as somewhat of an accomplishment, especially when they leave with two very important things intact: their pride and their library cards. Others have been known to mention "library" and "Olympic-caliber feat" in the same breath, saying a trip to the library requires more energy, stamina, and determination than the you-know-what Bunny.

"Oh, come on," you might be thinking. "What's the big deal? You go in, grab a book, and leave."

Well, maybe at one time. But now that you have tiny terrors in tow, going to the library is never that simple.   There's shushing under your breath. There's chasing without disrupting others. There's dodging oversized books. They're flying leaps to save the fish tank before it topples over. And, of course, there's making peace with all ten of the disgruntled librarians.

So you see, going to the library these days requires a unique set of skills—skills that will prevent you, by the way, from being thrown out by the seat of your sweats.

NEW-MOM LIBRARY SKILLS

The Shout-Whisper

Unless you want the little old ladies posted as guards throughout the library to crack you with their canes, you'll need to learn how to get your child's attention without disrupting the other readers. In other words, you'll need to learn how to combine two opposite methods of speaking—shouting and whispering.

Here's how to do it: Lower your chin to your neck, clench your teeth, squint your eyes, and loudly hiss your child's name. Like a prairie dog that senses danger, your child will be sniffing you out in no time.

The Small-Step Chase

When a child enters a library, they do not see what you see—a lovely place overflowing with free books. What their mischievous eyes see is a gigantic jungle of books, crawl spaces and chair forts, which is why they hit the floor running when you put them down. Since you, as a respectable member of the community, cannot break into a full-blown gallop as you race to apprehend your wildebeest, you'll need to perfect the Small-Step Chase.

Here's how to do it: Pinch your derriere tighter than a zip-lock bag, bend your knees as far as they'll go, and begin the chase using a series of small, quick, inconspicuous steps.

The Quick-Grip Reflex

Something happens to small children when they see an opened newspaper: They must whack it with all their might. Having said that—what can you expect to find in a library? Yes! Hundreds of opened newspapers. And what can you expect your little one to do? Right again! Belt them with a vengeance. Although steering clear of the newspaper section is your best bet, you won't always be able to do this. At times, you'll need to rely on the Quick-Grip Reflex.

Here's how to do it: Hold your arm in the ready position as you and your kiddo near the newspapers. The moment you see your little one cock his arm back, strike fast and grip that tiny wrist.

The Discreet-Fine-Paying Maneuver

Now that you're a mother, you can toss that "Never-Owed-a-Fine-in-My-Life" badge right out the window. Since motherhood and overdue books go together like check and checkbook, you better get used to filling your pockets before you head to Bookland. If your fine is huge, however, bordering on that humiliating Is-she-fit-to-be-a-mother? level, you might want to use the Discreet-Fine-Paying Maneuver.

Here's how to do it: The minute the library opens, rush to the checkout counter and throw a big book bag down—big enough to conceal what you're doing. Make sure no one you know is around, and then lean forward and whisper, "I'd like to know how much I owe; and I'd like you to use sign language to tell me."

The Grand-Slam Apology

Okay, so your one hour at the library turned into the worst 60 minutes of your life. How were you to know your daughter would bite clean through the librarian's support hose? How were you to know your son would nail a senior citizen with a spitball the size of Jupiter? Or how were you to know you'd lose track of your children only to find them moments later giggling like wicked hyenas from the "Librarians Only" bathroom? But things do not always go as planned, and so it's up to you to collect your dignity, take a deep breath, and do whatever it takes to stop that righteous librarian from shredding your card.

Here's how to do the Grand-Slam Apology: Stand behind the nearest podium you can find, grab the sides, and shout "QUIET!" When all eyes are upon you, remove your checkbook from your purse and say, "I'm truly sorry my children and I were so disruptive today. It won't happen again and, by the way, I hear the library needs new carpeting and would like to foot the entire bill."

PART 10

THE ANSWER TO THE QUESTION
MOMS GET ASKED MOST

FINALLY...

58.

WHAT DO MOTHERS DO ALL DAY?

Who killed JFK? Is Elvis really dead? And what do mothers do all day? These three questions have gripped the Western world for decades. And rightly so. No one seems to know the answer to any of them . . . particularly the last one.

So, what do mothers do all day?

If you're a Stay-at-Home Mom, you know. Boy, oh, boy, do you ever know. But if you're still toying with the idea of becoming a mother, maybe it would be a good idea to find out NOW.

Are you ready? Here goes for me, a typical mother of two.

I start my day heroically enough—armed with boundless energy and stoic determination, I produce an admirable list of all I plan to accomplish before noon: post office, grocery store, dry cleaners, bank, photomat, library. I proudly show my husband, who responds, "Go get 'em tiger."

This is my job, after all, and running thousands of errands in the shortest time possible is a feat I can proudly call my own.

Before Working Mothers could even think of making coffee, I'm out the door with my wailing three-year-old. "But me wanna watch Baaaaarney," can be heard blocks from my home as I desperately pacify my child with, "But pumpkin, we can have a doughnut at the grocery store, a lollipop at the bank, gumballs at the dry cleaners, and Smarties at the photomat. Doesn't that sound just supercali-expialidocious?"

My day, however, does not go as expected. My son fills his pants at the grocery store, knocks over a display at the photomat, and calls me a "big poopie head" at the bank. Defeated, I return home—a spent and exhausted Stay-at-Home Mom.

Dragging my weary body inside, I immediately spot billions of black ants crawling along the baseboard. The crisis jogs me back to the reality of my chore-oriented day, and I tackle the nuisance with alarming speed. The task, picayune to some, fortifies me with new energy.

Changing a diaper with one hand and reading *Goodnight Moon* with the other, I vacuum with my left foot and dust with my right. My mind races to future missions: fixing lunch, making coffee, removing that big vomit stain, fixing snacks, making more coffee, removing other big and equally disgusting stains—FOOD, COFFEE, STAINS—FOOD, COFFEE, STAINS.

My son's high-spirited giggle interrupts my illustrious train of thought. What feels wet? I wonder. When I see what he's done to the front of my shirt, I have no choice but to laugh, too. He giggles harder and sticks a chubby foot in my face to be tickled. I feel overwhelmed with love and decide to chuck my chore list right out the window. We spend the next few hours productively goofing off.

I hear the noon siren and am reminded of the flirting, laughing, livin'-it-up lunch crowd. I was once part of that commotion. A semi-jealous tear wells in the corner of my eye. I can almost taste the gourmet soup du jour as I gag down a bowl of Curly Noodle with my child. Flicking a carrot piece at the window, I repeat my stay-at-home mantra:

> *I am one of the lucky few,*
> *I am one of the lucky few,*
> *I feel like a big ducky doo.*

A putrid odor directs me to change another diaper, my fifth since this morning. I take a solemn moment and pray for the day when my toddler is potty trained.

I soon put my wide-awake child down for a nap. He refuses. I beg. He climbs out. I beg some more. Finally, after a grueling episode that reduces us both to tears, he falls asleep, and I crawl out of the room on my hands and knees. It is now two o'clock. I have been awake for eight hours and have yet to crack the morning paper. My first grader is due home at three.

Like a glittering oasis of time, a golden hour dangles above me. I toy with exercising to an aerobics tape (too demanding). I ponder updating my photo album (too overwhelming). I consider cleaning the toilets (too disgusting). I contemplate learning Italian (far too ambitious).

In the end and with only ten minutes of my precious hour left, I call my mother who, as things would have it, can't talk anyway— she's in the middle of a thrilling game of bridge.

A huge fly lands on the kitchen table. I kill it with shocking gusto. The noise awakens my sleeping child at the very moment my tireless first grader bursts through the door demanding all kinds of things: a snack, money for a book order, new sneaks, more glue, and instant playmates.

Before I can collect my wits, the afternoon unfolds into a frenzied maelstrom of preparing snacks, sweeping crumbs, soothing tears, reading books, picking up, dodging toys, tossing balls, changing diapers, making dinner, drinking coffee, and sweeping more crumbs.

After dinner, I close my eyes for a fraction of a second and replay the same delirious fantasy I've been visualizing for months. No, it's not the one where I've got a nationally syndicated Helpful Hints column. And no, it's not the one where Yan arrives to give my aching body a Swedish massage. It's the one where the Goodnight Fairy sweeps into my home and puts my cranky children to bed. That one.

Somewhere between eight and nine o'clock, after undergoing a battery of routines, my children succumb to the bodily function that presents them at their very best: sleep. I study their darling faces and wonder why it can't always be so.

I stagger out of their room, and like a boxer who refuses to be TKO'd, I finish the dishes, pack lunches, sort laundry, glance at the paper, wrap a birthday present, chat with my husband, drink cold coffee, and sweep final crumbs.

An alarming pressure fills me. Oh-my-God! It is now and only now that I realize something significant that I have forgotten to do all day—PEE.

❊   ❊   ❊

Infant Potty Training:
A Gentle and Primeval Method
Adapted to Modern Living

500 pages
$19.50